Spirit
Untethered

---

*A Psychotherapist's Journey
from Terminal Cancer
to Seeing the Dead*

SUZANNE GRACE MAIDEN

BALBOA
PRESS
A DIVISION OF HAY HOUSE

Copyright © 2018 Suzanne Grace Maiden.

All rights reserved. No part of this book may be used or reproduced by any means, graphic, electronic, or mechanical, including photocopying, recording, taping or by any information storage retrieval system without the written permission of the author except in the case of brief quotations embodied in critical articles and reviews.

This book is a work of non-fiction. Unless otherwise noted, the author and the publisher make no explicit guarantees as to the accuracy of the information contained in this book and in some cases, names of people and places have been altered to protect their privacy.

Balboa Press books may be ordered through booksellers or by contacting:

Balboa Press
A Division of Hay House
1663 Liberty Drive
Bloomington, IN 47403
www.balboapress.com
1 (877) 407-4847

Because of the dynamic nature of the Internet, any web addresses or links contained in this book may have changed since publication and may no longer be valid. The views expressed in this work are solely those of the author and do not necessarily reflect the views of the publisher, and the publisher hereby disclaims any responsibility for them.

The author of this book does not dispense medical advice or prescribe the use of any technique as a form of treatment for physical, emotional, or medical problems without the advice of a physician, either directly or indirectly. The intent of the author is only to offer information of a general nature to help you in your quest for emotional and spiritual well-being. In the event you use any of the information in this book for yourself, which is your constitutional right, the author and the publisher assume no responsibility for your actions.

Any people depicted in stock imagery provided by Getty Images are models, and such images are being used for illustrative purposes only. Certain stock imagery © Getty Images.

Print information available on the last page.

ISBN: 978-1-9822-0652-9 (sc)
ISBN: 978-1-9822-0654-3 (hc)
ISBN: 978-1-9822-0653-6 (e)

Library of Congress Control Number: 2018907456

Balboa Press rev. date: 10/29/2018

CONTENTS

Foreword by Barry Williams, PsyD ix
Introduction by Marjorie Woollacott, PhD xv

Chapter 1	The Call 1
Chapter 2	First Contact 18
Chapter 3	Diagnosis: Terminal Cancer 31
Chapter 4	The Naked Medium 44
Chapter 5	Animal Spirits 55
Chapter 6	Discouraging Friends and Unexpected Support 68
Chapter 7	Spirit Is Relentless 82
Chapter 8	Believe 92
Chapter 9	Signs 105

DEDICATION

For my heavenly father.
And, for Spirits who gifted me with concrete evidence
and demonstrated that death is an illusion.
May these pages help broken hearts heal.

FOREWORD
by Barry Williams, PsyD

I met Suzanne and became her analyst seventeen years ago. At the time, she was still recovering from a major surgery to remove a large, deadly sarcoma from her midsection. Though her initial prognosis was somewhat optimistic, it went sharply downhill statistically after five years, and presently, she is living with a stage IV cancer diagnosis. The fact that she is still alive, vital, creative, and enthusiastic, filled with an understanding and wisdom about life, death, love, and meaning, is due in no small part to her spiritual experiences: namely, the unfolding revelation of the presence of the spirit world and the message of love and the continuity of life and death that she has been asked to convey.

I have had the privilege to bear witness to Suzanne's deep, intense, and authentic journey of transformation—which has opened her inner eyes, ears, and heart to their living presence of the other world and its spirit inhabitants. Facing the grimmest diagnosis that pushed her beyond the threshold of the personal life, she has been opened to the message of enduring love. These unbidden messages come through to her and give life meaning, hope, and integrity; they provide great continuity and relatedness with all things. Suzanne's process certainly encompasses what C. G. Jung referred to as the *process of individuation*.

A sure sign what Jung called this *process of individuation* is working in your life is the lack of clear, discernable pathways between where you started in childhood regarding your family and where you find yourself as an adult. That refining process of becoming profoundly and uniquely *who you most inwardly are* often requires you to leave behind old assumptions and expectations of life—particularly those that were placed on you by outer realities such as family, society, education, church, or culture. You do this in order to follow another path—another voice—which urges you to move toward and claim your truer nature.

Both Suzanne's life story and this book that catalogues her journey invite us to move our awareness out of its comfortable home and into an expanded world. Within this world, the spirits of our ancestors want to find a way to communicate with us. They want to deliver important messages about the nature of life, death, and love. If we tend to make the mistake of thinking life is concrete, sensate, and rational, or that what you see is what you get, we may miss it. We may miss the miracles right in front of us because they cannot be defined by the rational and thinking mind.

We live in a spirit-filled universe whether we know it or not, or whether we want to know it or not. It can reveal itself to us from the outside, objectively through our perceptions, or inwardly, through intuition, dreams, an inner journey—or, in Suzanne's case, the increasingly audible voices of the spirit world.

Oftentimes, these abilities begin with sacrifice and an initiatory process. For Suzanne, this involved a set of shocking traumatic deaths followed by nearly two decades of living with an ongoing, unfolding, metastatic cancer. These events took her out of her old life and forced her into a reality that she did not ask for or want.

Her personal story is noteworthy in itself, but what is truly extraordinary is the measure to which a mythic or archetypal pattern plays itself out through her, allowing, motivating, and defining her journey from what she would describe as a "country club housewife" to one who sees, one who hears, one who bridges the worlds of life and death, matter and spirit, one who brings the message that our waking, anxious world is so hungry to hear.

I believe it is safe to say that Suzanne's gift of communication with the world of the dead derives in large part from her dominant dream motif. She has given me permission to reveal that she often dreams about snakes, and I think this tells a lot about her experience. Serpent symbolism is extensive and mysterious and goes in many different directions at once—it could indicate healing, aspects of the goddess, instinctual energies, guarding the treasure, the world from below, and much, much more. In this case, I believe the motifs of temptation, wisdom, and the primordial aspects of nature are the most important.

The serpent in the biblical Garden story, from a psychological perspective, is about the invitation toward consciousness. This consciousness is necessary for development and is in fact part of the unfolding drama of how the human world interacts with the reality of the divine world. The snakes in Suzanne's dreams represent a similar calling that beckons her out of a state of unconsciousness and toward the path she is to follow, no matter the difficulty or the hardships. Seen from this angle, Suzanne's gift is not "the devil's work"—though some have suggested as much. Rather, it is an invitation to come into relationship with mystery.

Another aspect of the serpent imagery that is important here is wisdom. The wisdom of the serpent is the wisdom of nature. What the serpent knows is what nature knows, what the primordial unconscious knows. It has to do with an understanding that is so far beyond human cognition that it appears in the guise of a being that is nearly incomprehensible to humans. This being holds crucial knowledge that cannot be articulated. This knowledge is the third important aspect of serpent symbolism to help understand Suzanne's gift and calling. We might call it an embodiment of the knowledge of the way things are. The dreams of snakes are thus an expression of a reality that seems mysterious, uncanny, or even frightening but which indicates that we have arrived at a deeper understanding than the rational mind can attain. The serpent world comes over and over to express to the dreamer what she cannot know but must relate to, and often by threatening her life.

The archetypal energies and patterns of initiation also play an important role in Suzanne's journey. Individuation requires a series of initiations throughout life. Initiation always entails a separation from a static, accustomed life, the crossing of a threshold, and a reincorporation into a new status of consciousness. The initiate possesses a new level of wisdom that arises from the suffering this process entails, and this wisdom serves to change their very identity. Of course, Suzanne's cancer has been a strong and singular motivating agent of initiation for her. It has lifted her out of her old identity; dismembered her both through surgeries and through a profound humbling by a disorienting, threshold liminality; and pieced her back together, not in the body so much as in her new orientation to the other world of the talking spirits.

What the serpents know cannot be transmitted through her until she crosses the threshold of the suffering of what she faces as an embodied being. The veil could not have been thinned enough for her to see and hear the messages of the dead had she not left her old corporeal reality and been forced into a new one. It is as if the spirits, like a dream, came to her unbidden, perhaps both pushing her across the threshold and seizing upon her when she emerged, so as to make her one of them; both allowing and demanding that she become a "spirit speaker," the instrument of a message it is now time to hear.

Another helpful concept for an appreciation of Suzanne's development as one who sees is the mythic theme of the hero's journey. This journey of ego development that separates and differentiates the hero from the unconscious begins with a call to transformation. If the call is accepted, there is a passage through ordeals and ultimately the acquisition of the treasure of life. A deeper understanding of the hero's journey, seen and experienced as a personal struggle, is the dawning awareness that you are being initiated by forces that are much greater than your ability to understand them. If you surrender and submit to this deeper process, another world opens to you, and it holds the promise of great meaning and fulfillment.

This is the nature of Suzanne's path. Certainly, her hero's journey to acquire her credentials as a therapist moved from her ordinary reality, though her studies at Pacifica Graduate Institute for a master's degree, and on to licensure. But at the same time, she lived a hero's journey through her confrontation with another force—one with whom she could not negotiate, no matter how much she doubted or struggled or denied it. It pushed her and nudged her even as she tried to keep her inner spirit story secret. Cancer pushed her, dreams pushed her, her emerging abilities and gifts as a therapist pushed her, and all the while, the spirit world would not leave her alone.

In the end, her true hero's journey has been her willingness to submit to an initiation she was helpless to avoid. It's as if she'd made a bargain: if she fought the call, it would kill her, and if she submitted to it, it would keep her alive and give her a new life—but in either case, it would be the end of the only life she'd known.

Her ability to hear that message has only resulted from her surrender to a process that promised to take her life—but which, at the same time, seems to be preserving it, perhaps even only for the sake passing the message along. For the most part, we cannot understand the demands that the totality of our being, the God nature of our lives, or the spirit world makes on us. We can only bow to the enormity and trust deeply that the path we've been set upon is the crucial path of our individuation journey; the one that promises us our destiny and that makes us into who we most inwardly are.

Spirit's consistent message to Suzanne, and therefore to all of us, is actually quite simple: death itself is illusory. Love binds us all together. It is love that tethers us through the great cycle of life. The messages contained in the following pages are for all who question the cyclical nature of life and death, including the greatest question of all: if life continues after the body dies.

Barry S. Williams, M. Div., PsyD
Diplomate Jungian Analyst
Mara`akame

INTRODUCTION
by Marjorie Woollacott, PhD

I first met Suzanne Maiden at the International Association for Near-Death Studies (IANDS) Conference in Colorado in August 2017, where I heard the story of how she awakened to her own psychic and mediumship abilities. I was intrigued. How surprising it is, at this point in my life, to find myself intrigued—rather than dismissing such an account out of hand, as I would have done years ago. Before I had my own spiritual awakening, I was in a state of absolute certainty about the material basis of life and dismissed paranormal experiences such as those found in meditation and mediumship.

You may be wondering why Suzanne asked me, a neuroscientist, to write an introduction to her book—and why would I consider it. As a result of my own spiritual journey, I now have great uncertainty about the material basis of reality and curiosity about paranormal or spiritual phenomena. I have learned that it is only when we are uncertain about aspects of reality that we are curious enough to be intrigued by other possibilities.

As I noted above, I am a neuroscientist, specializing in rehabilitation medicine, and I was a materialist and an atheist at the beginning of my career. I remember being at family reunions when I was in high school and college, talking to my uncle, who had graduated from Cal Tech and was a physicist, laughing together about the weak-minded people in our family who were spiritually oriented. Then, when I was thirty years old, my sister invited me to a retreat given by a meditation master. In that retreat, I had a spiritual awakening that shifted my worldview 180 degrees. For the first time, I had the experience of energy radiating from within my heart, filling my entire being. It felt like nectar, like pure love flowing through me. I felt that I was truly home for the first time in my life, and that home was my heart. Since that time, as I have continued to meditate, I have felt the strong intention to expand my scientific worldview so that I could fit the realm of spirituality within it. And I have begun to research meditation and other spiritual experiences from both a scientific point of view and from the realm of first-person experiences.

As I read *Spirit Untethered*, new understandings about the awakening of our spiritual nature became clear to me. Suzanne's conclusions in some ways mirror my own. For example, through her experiences with grief, cancer, and ultimately mediumship, Suzanne came to the clear understanding that we are not these bodies—rather, the body is just the vessel the soul uses for a short time. This same insight came to me in my first meditation experience, when I felt the energy radiating from my heart and heard the words inside, "I'm home, I'm home. My heart is my home." I knew at a deep level that I was not this body, that I was much more than this. And that this essence, the energy of my "heart," would not vanish when the body died.

Most of the chapters of Suzanne's book are related to her growing awakening and refining of this ability to hear spirits and to share their communications with their loved ones on earth. As a neuroscientist, I was fascinated to read them. This is partly because this has long been considered by neuroscientists as an area that is totally foreign to the realm of scientific study. When I was first writing my book about my own spiritual awakening, *Infinite Awareness: The Awakening of a Scientific Mind*, I did not even explore the area of mediumship. In part, I was leery of it, remembering frightening movies from my childhood about exorcism.

But when my scientific curiosity led me to explore peer-reviewed research on mediumship, I found that there is substantial evidence-based research published in peer-reviewed journals giving results indicating that mediums are able to communicate valid information about persons who have died that could not be known by the medium him or herself. For example, in a study by Emily Williams and Diane Arcangel (*J Nerv Ment Dis* 2011), highly significant results were found. In this controlled study, mediums provided readings about certain deceased persons to a proxy sitter, and the real sitter then blindly rated this reading that was intended for them, along with other control readings related to other people. I continue to seek out research in this realm, much of which is still emerging as the scientific community slowly opens to these ideas.

I thus began exploring Suzanne's book, *Spirit Untethered*, with real curiosity and interest in the phenomenon. Through this exploration, my understanding of the value of mediumship has increased. I now see not only the possibility of the authenticity of mediumship, but the promise that possibility holds: that our loved ones really care about our well-being, and will do anything they can to help nurture us in our growth as human beings.

As you read *Spirit Untethered*, I believe you will find that Suzanne's stories have an energetic effect on the heart. This effect serves to open us more and more to the possibilities of this nurturing benevolent communication, not only with spirits from the other side but with animals and our own spirit guides, who want only the best for us. May reading this book enrich your life as it did mine.

Marjorie Woollacott, PhD and author

ACKNOWLEDGMENTS

Spirit Untethered begged to be born and shared with the masses. Since her inception, people from around the world requested sample chapters – their positive responses kept my fingers tapping out stories on my laptop. Thank you to those of you who cheered this work forward. I believe in this work so much that I willingly pushed myself through two back reconstructions to remove tumors on my spine - rounds of radiation – and more chemotherapy to bring these true stories to publication. And, I had tremendous help. Through the tireless sacrifices of others I completed a dream.

First, to my husband Robin. You are my North Star – you shine light when all I can see is darkness. You steady my gait when my feet falter. You hold my hand and offer loving words of reassurance. You learned to cook delicious and healthy food to keep my body strong. You emptied dozens of vomit-filled basins. Thank you my darling for sharing this lifetime with me. Thank you for holding both my hand and my heart. I love you.

To our beautiful son Max. You continue to bring endless uproarious laughter. Your delightful presence adds merriment into our familial fold. I treasure you. What a privilege it is to be your mother. Thank you, honey, for supporting me all throughout this work. I love you.

To my parents. Your unyielding belief in this work provided the spring board for me to jump. To my father: you modeled perseverance. To my mother: you modeled compassion. The union of both perseverance and compassion created silver wings for me to soar. I love you.

To my three brothers. Each of you influenced me in profound ways. To my youngest brother James, or "Georgie." You emotionally coached me all the way. Georgie your cheerleading via daily texts and phone calls encouraged me. I love all of you.

To The Divas: Amy Rissier, Carrie Runnals, Julie Karneboge and Sharon Martin. You helped keep me alive when cancer tried to kill me. You shared shifts at the hospital to ensure I was well looked after. You brought dinners and smoothies and ginger ale and homemade soups. You ran errands, dried my tears – and supported me – literally and figuratively. I hold you each in my heart with loving gratitude.

To Candy P. You helped me when I couldn't help myself – your faithful friendship is a true gift.

To my three, lifelong spirit-sisters. You have each suffered tremendous shock loss of a beloved. Katherine Martinez, for over 30 years you never stopped believing in me. Our spirit-sister bond is stronger than titanium. Debbie Garratt, you ushered me into the world of psychic phenomenon and mediumship. Jenny Suzumoto, my fairy friend. You ploughed through so many pages and paragraphs when I felt stuck. Your lovely suggestions made my writing stronger.

To my editor, Chandika Devi. You Chandika, are a writer's dream. You knew when to push me and when to pause. To kn literary, I recommend your services to anyone thinking about writing a book. You are terrific!

To my colleagues. All of you patiently listened when I bounced in our office and excitedly shared about my latest Spirit contact. Even now – you still listen with love.

To all of my Spiritual teachers: Lou B., Kathy S., Jerry H., Barry W., and Francis D. You each arrived precisely at the right moment. Each of you contributed to my development as a psychic-medium. You're influence is immeasurable. I love you all.

To Louise Hay. Although we never met in this time-space dimension, I have a strong feeling we will connect again across the veil. Thank you for having the chutzpah to start a publishing company - Hay House. What a gift to the entire collective! Thanks to Hay House who took a chance on me and this work. I am indebted to you for this opportunity.

Finally, to Brian and Carole Weiss. Brian, with a single sentence - you changed the trajectory of my life. I listened. I heeded your words. This book is the result of our discussion. Carole, your gentle words somehow arrived at the precise moment I needed. Thank you for your kindness.

HOW DO I LOVE THEE?

How do I love thee? Let me count the ways.
I love thee to the depth and breadth and height
My soul can reach, when feeling out of sight
For the ends of being and ideal grace.
I love the to the level of every day's
Most quiet need, by sun and candle-light.
I love thee freely, as men strive for right.
I love thee purely, as they turn from praise.
I love thee with the passion put to use
In my old griefs, and with my childhood's faith.
I love thee with a love I seemed to lose
With my lost saints. I love thee with the breadth,
Smiles, tears, of all my life; and, if God choose,
I shall love thee better after death.

—Elizabeth Barrett Browning, 1806-1861

CHAPTER 1

The Call

> You must give up the life you planned in order to have the life that is waiting for you.
>
> —*Joseph Campbell*

Six months before I was diagnosed with terminal cancer, I started to see dead people—or spirits. As of this writing, four years have passed. As Campbell said, we have to give up one life to receive another. And this is true. Through forcing me to give up so much, all of the world conspired to convert me, an average housewife and mother, to a psychic medium. They converted me so that I could write these words—their message to you. *We never die. We merely depart our physical bodies. Invisible forces that anchored us to the body release, and the intact Spirit finds a home on a new plane just a hairsbreadth away from this one.*

In stubborn ignorance, I fought my own psychic and mediumistic gifts for two reasons. First, I didn't believe I actually had this gift, and second, I was afraid. I was afraid of being labeled a charlatan or—worse—being accused of doing something that was not of God. Eventually, I yielded. Eventually, I learned. As of this writing, my learning process continues. I know that I shall always be a disciple of life. In the meantime, I'm still working to keep my own body going. One of the biggest motivations for being here is this: I fight to stay alive so that I can not only tell you we never die but also demonstrate it through evidential mediumship.

But no one arrives at their sacred destination unscathed. Most of us arrive war-weary and battle-scarred. For some people, physical survival itself feels like a miraculous accomplishment, let alone arriving with newfound spiritual enlightenment. It wasn't just the cancer itself that made space for this opening; I also had to face my own grief to develop the gift that allows me to share this story.

Before I could embrace my psychic and mediumistic gifts, my life blew up in a series of six metaphorical bombs designed to provide me with a divine, custom-created course correction. It worked. Under siege, agonizing events held me captive. My soul stretched to her furthest limits. If a soul could have physical stretch marks, mine would run jagged and red across my being—proof of how I've had to stretch and grow to survive. But this was all part of my spiritual education. Eventually, these painful lessons pointed the way across the veil—the place where Spirit dwells.

The first bomb was more like a hand grenade. While hand grenades can make a scary impact, they are not the biggest warhead in the arsenal—though they sometimes forewarn that bigger bombs will arrive. When this hand grenade struck, I did not know what was to come.

Nelly was my mother-in-law, and Nicole was her cousin. The two grew up together in France in the post-WWII era. Both Nicole and Nelly married American servicemen, and decades later, when their husbands retired from the military, everyone ended up living in Huntsville, Alabama. Nicole was a healthy, middle-aged woman and more gregarious than my mother-in-law. They had a sisterly relationship complete with mild competition, jealousy, and arguments. But love always won.

Spirit Untethered

Everyone, including Nelly and me, was shocked when Nicole died suddenly from a heart attack. I went to assist Nelly with funeral preparations. This was my first experience with sudden death, and I had been very lucky because I was already thirty-one years old.

We entered the empty church where Nicole's funeral service was scheduled. Nelly dressed her tall, slender body in elegant styles. Nobody had better couture than my French mother-in-law. When we were together, I had to up my fashion game. Our high-heeled feet made *click-click-click* sounds on the church floor as we walked with purpose. In a mindless mumble, I confessed, "I feel rather anxious. Uh, well, I've never seen a corpse before." The idea creeped me out. My mother-in-law confidently reassured me it would be okay. And as it turned out, it was; I managed to get through the preparations and the full funeral service without once seeing the corpse.

Although I escaped viewing Nicole's corpse, the universe scripted a much more painful plot. When I confided to Nelly that I had never seen a corpse, I had no idea that the first corpse I was destined to see would be her own! But before that could happen, the second bomb exploded. This one was like a nuclear bomb.

His foot, part of his torso, and one of his hands were returned to us. His mangled corpse was flown back in a too shiny, black, already sealed coffin. My thirty-seven-year-old brother, Rob, was dead.

Rob, a mechanical engineer, and his boss worked for Ingersoll Milling Machine Company. They had flown from Chicago to Indianapolis for a quick business meeting. Their meeting went well, so they wrapped up early, enabling them to change their flight and arrive home sooner. It was a cruel turn; they thought they would get back to Chicago earlier, and indeed they did—but not alive.

The American Eagle ATR-72 aircraft carried a full load of passengers and crew. As Flight 4184 approached Chicago's

O'Hare Airport, air traffic control instructed them to hold. As the ATR-72 flew in big circles, ice built on the wings. The ATR-72 was instructed to hold between 8,000 and 10,000 feet, the ideal altitude for ice formation. This scenario is usually safe because airplane wings are fitted with deicing boots. When ice forms, a device on the leading edge of the wing inflates and breaks the ice up. It's an effective system, unless the deicing boots are not big enough for the wing size. The deicing boots for the ATR-72 were too small. Not just for that particular ATR-72 but for the entire fleet. And American Airlines knew it. Europe banned ATR-72s because they had too many fatal incidents in icing conditions. So American Airlines purchased the banned ATR-72 at bargain-basement prices. *They purchased these planes with full knowledge of their crash history.*

Ten more minutes remained until Flight 4184 was cleared to land. The captain noted to the copilot that he had seen that a portion of the wing had some ice. But neither could see the rest of the ice on the wings. What happened next is best described in Stephen Frederick's 1996 book, *Unheeded Warning*.

> The aircraft rolled violently to the right, stopping at a 77-degree, right-wing-down position. Everyone aboard the aircraft was tossed to the left and then quickly to the right as G-forces caught up ... Neither pilot could have known what was happening to the aircraft ... Flight 4184 was falling at 30,000 feet per minute ... The aircraft exceeded 373 knots. G-forces reached 5.2 and the aircraft broke. The outer 10 feet of both wings and the horizontal tail separated from the airliner. The aircraft smashed the ground and disintegrated into pieces. The cockpit area microphone picked up a loud crunching sound ... The quiet returned and the wind and rain were audible again.

After the ATR-72 crashed, the site was immediately cordoned off. A critical response team was assembled and sent to recover remains. The team trudged through miles of soybean fields dotted with mangled aircraft debris and mutilated bodies. Their gruesome task was to locate and collect body parts. This part of crash recovery is called "bag and tag." I accidentally saw some of this process on the nightly news. An aerial newscast filmed the crash site. In revulsion, I watched people in biohazard suits place colored flags next to human body parts and broken aircraft. It looked surreal. I stood up. I walked closer to the television. I scanned the screen to look for my brother. *Anything.* This horror film held me captive. The aerial journalist seemed excited to explain the process.

It turns out that when human remains are bagged and tagged, they get a free ride to a makeshift morgue. In this case, that instant morgue was an empty local high school. A team of coroners from Washington, DC, arrived. They performed tissue typing in an effort to match human remains with dental records. Their goal was to identify every passenger and crew member who perished. The entire town of Roselawn, Indiana, mourned. Because parts of bodies and aircraft were scattered across a five-mile radius, anyone could find anything anywhere. What a perfect backdrop for a horror flick. Fate signed its unique signature to this event. It just so happened to be Halloween Day, 1994.

Rob's lovely wife and two young sons were as broken apart as that airplane. Our parents never fully recovered. The boys grew up, Rob's wife remarried, and life dramatically changed for our family. Until this point in my life, I hadn't known much about death; it never had touched me deeply. But when death did touch me, it nearly took me with it.

After my brother's death, I became unstable. My weight plummeted to an unhealthy level because I could not make food go down my throat. I was exhausted, but sleep eluded me. I cut off all of my curly blonde hair and dyed it dark auburn. And to round out this glamorous vision, I subconsciously pulled out all of my eyelashes. I drank too much. I considered suicide. I sank deeply into the dark abyss of suffering.

Grief inhabited me, and I inhabited grief. Like Siamese twins, we seemed permanently joined. My grief forced me to put my life on hold and take a leave of absence from graduate school. I wanted evidence that my brother was okay. I wanted proof that death is an illusion and that love creates continued bonds. I searched for verifiable psychic mediums. I asked people who I thought would be receptive to my question and made many phone calls to find someone who could authentically communicate with the dead. I read every book I could get a hold of on the subject of life after death and mediums. So did my mother. Together, we were on a sacred hunt to find the real deal. Our hope was that someone could provide us with detailed, specific evidence that would prove—without a doubt—that Rob was still alive in spiritual form.

Together, we identified several mediums who seemed sincere and did deliver some accurate data. But my skepticism kept me from completely believing. My need to understand what happens after death and that we really never die drove me toward increased neurotic behavior. I became obsessed with my search. It was as if I could not stop dialing-a-medium to prove that life after death is real. Because my husband and I did not have any children yet, and I was on leave from graduate school, I had abundant time. Sometimes, when my husband, Robin, returned home after work and asked me what I had been doing with my day, I was too ashamed to answer. I collected the names and contact information of possible psychic/mediums in a logbook, which I kept hidden from him. This was far more indicative of my own shame and embarrassment than anything else; as I later found out, Robin was very supportive, and the need to hide my interest in mediumship was purely my own.

Thanksgiving arrived, and my family gathered in somber observance. Then, it was as if the calendar had wings, and Christmas arrived too soon. My husband and I departed Chicago and flew south to Huntsville, Alabama, to spend Christmas with his family. Nelly, my mother-in-law, worked hard to create a joyful holiday for us. Everything was lovely. But grief hijacked my joy. Without permission or warning, tears would suddenly spill from my eyes like a swollen river floods its banks. I felt like the walking dead—though I did not know then that the dead were walking with me. Literally.

Here's the truth of the matter: *in Spirit form, your loved one does everything and anything they can to grab your attention in an effort to comfort you.* Through this grief, my brother, Rob, was trying to grab ahold of me. I know this because Spirit has shown me, over and over again. But before these truths were demonstrated to me, I had more growing pains to endure. Rob's death called my attention but not enough of it; I still needed to be broken wide open.

Gloomy winter passed. Spring arrived—and so did my hope. I began to reengage with life. Part of my survival strategy included researching everything on death, the grieving process, and evidence of life after death. I engaged the help of a therapist who was knowledgeable about grief, and emotional stability felt just around the corner. I was ready to restart graduate school in the fall, just a few weeks away.

Before academic responsibilities resumed, my husband and I invited his parents to visit us. We all loved water activities, and we were eager to take them for a weekend out on our boat. I also wanted to prove to Nelly that I was emotionally mending. The last time we were together was the disastrous Christmas six months prior, when I was in the initial phases of my grief. Everyone anticipated the upcoming visit. It was all planned.

As it turned out, a third bomb was headed our way. Nelly never made her visit. Instead, Nelly was murdered.

Less than a year after we arranged Nicole's funeral, and eight months after my brother's plane went down, Nelly was shot in the head. She worked in a quaint boutique owned by her best friend. That July day, the Alabama heat and humidity made people's clothes come off. Nelly, chatting on the phone, told the person on the other end that she was concerned. She could see through the window that a man in a leather jacket was approaching the store, and who would wear a leather jacket in such heat? The jacket concealed his hand. His hand held a gun. Nelly ran toward the back door, but two other accomplices blocked her departure.

These men thought the boutique had a safe full of cash, but they were wrong. It wasn't just that this shop did not have much cash; it did not even have a safe. Somebody did not do their homework. The men got mad. They roughed Nelly up. In a final effort to force her to disclose the location of the nonexistent safe, one of the men shoved a gun barrel to the back of her head. Whether intentional or not, the gun discharged. The bullet penetrated her brain and exited her jaw. Nelly was dead.

How can a single bullet feel as big as a bomb?

The fatal gunshot created facial trauma. The funeral home sensitively draped a cloth over Nelly's face. Her familiar frame lay on the funeral home's gurney. Her lovely hands—those hands that previously carried so much life as they prepared delicious meals and wrapped gifts for us—lay uncannily still, but her hallmark manicure appeared fresh. Fringes of her black hair peaked out beneath the facial cloth. As my eyes scanned her corpse, I wanted her to know that we loved her. My husband, Robin, needed to see his mother's face one last time. He needed to see where she was shot. He needed to lift up the cloth that masked his mother's fatal gunshot wound. I could not emotionally handle seeing this type of trauma—so I opted to step out of the room. When I stepped out of the modern crypt that held Nelly's corpse, this gave my husband private time to witness the exact area the bullet had entered her head and exited her jaw. This was something he needed to see. He needed to have private time with her.

Removing her facial cloth to view her face was one of the hardest things my husband ever did. Life became forever defined as before or after his mother was killed. Death posts a permanent mark on a survivor's calendar. This is how it was for him.

But I couldn't connect with Nelly because her lifeless body felt like a vacant house. It felt empty. Nelly was not in her body. Her energy was gone. In that nanosecond, I got it. I. Got. It! *We are not our bodies. Our body is just the vessel our soul temporarily borrows. The body dies; the soul continues. I get it!* But this knowledge did not stop me from ever grieving again.

The best present Nelly ever gave to me was the privilege to see her corpse. Seeing Nelly's corpse taught me that death is an illusion. The very thing I had avoided doing—seeing a corpse—ended up bringing me a divine gift. My greatest teacher was the sum of these experiences. My ignorant arrogance needed to be blown up and reconstructed before I could understand. I needed first to be able to fathom the depth of emotional pain people endure when their beloved dies. I needed a whopper of a course correction toward The Call—toward my sacred destiny. I needed bombs to irrevocably blow up my life and force me onto a new path. Before I would ever be blessed with seeing spirits, I was deconstructed to be reconstructed. A kinder, more patient, more tolerant Suzanne emerged. Like a lotus blossom erupts from mud, tapping its roots deep down into the muck. And when I eventually emerged from the murky depths of agonizing grief, my soul softened, and I felt a surge of loving compassion for all people.

Life and death. Death and life. My grandmother Grace used to say: "Life and death always come in threes. When one person dies, be ready, because you'll hear about two more. If one baby is born, you'll find out that two more women are expecting." That sounded like a silly old wives' tale. But my grandma knew some stuff. Three weeks after Nelly's murder and just months after Rob's death, I discovered I was pregnant.

We had a beautiful, healthy baby boy. As our son grew, I continued my research on shock loss, grief, and life after death. I volunteered as a lay therapist until I eventually returned to graduate school. When I became a licensed psychotherapist, I tailored my practice toward grief; I published on sudden-death grief, I spoke as a keynote speaker to teach other health care providers to help educate them on the process, and I started a grief support group at a local church. I thought this was The Call, the whole call. I erroneously thought that now I had found my life's purpose. "Not so fast," said the universe; unbidden, my next initiation beckoned me. I was about to be introduced to what is clinically called *anticipatory death*. This time, it was my own life that was suspended between two worlds.

We had just celebrated our son's fourth birthday. My abdomen hurt. Twelve months of doctor's visits found nothing. Then my abdominal pain escalated. I called my local internist and diagnosed myself with probable appendicitis. The doctor agreed. But testing revealed a nine-centimeter cancerous tumor attached to my spine, right iliac crest, and front psoas muscle. That tumor looked like a pork tenderloin in my gut. Things happened fast.

A month of radiation left me tired and nauseated. That was the first part of treatment. Our four-year-old son was shuffled around to my family and local friends. Surgery followed. The team sliced me open from my spine, over my hip, to the groin; thirteen inches and 150 staples later, they got the entire tumor. Recovery felt very long. But recover I did. My motivation stood right before me in his nightly pull-ups and loose blond curls. Our son clung to me as if he somehow understood the possibility of his mother dying. His chubby face and thighs sustained me. This was the moment when I begged God to save me.

Death and I brokered a deal: if I were permitted to see my son grow up and graduate high school, then I would commit to being of greater service to the collective. Death held that bargain but remained in the shadows. I healed. I vowed to make my life more useful and do even more acts of service. For a decade before these events, and before I became a mother, I donated hundreds of hours volunteering for various nonprofit groups. First, I worked with battered women; second, homeless children; and third, inner-city youth.

When I volunteered for battered women, I worked the crisis hotline and support groups. I joined the Junior League of Atlanta and worked one day per week with children in state custody. I drove into the city and spent extra time with these children, interacting with them through reading, drawing, making crafts, or sometimes just rocking a child.

During one of those times during the Christmas season, I made monogrammed stockings for each child and stuffed it with toys and candy. We were pretty broke at the time, so I borrowed a Santa suit from my hair dresser. That suit must have been made to fit a miniature elf, because when my 6'4" husband put it on, I doubled over in heaves of laughter—the suit was too tight and too short. He wore it anyway and never complained. We drove our old silver Oldsmobile, nicknamed "the silver bomb," to the state facility. Across the parking lot from the children's unit was the residential unit for psychotic patients. Some psychotic patients watched us and began to shout obscenities at "Santa" and me—they laughed and laughed at his too-small Santa Claus suit. We looked ridiculous. We laughed along with them.

When that state facility closed, I shifted my efforts to work with inner-city high schoolers who were identified as at-risk youth. They were a tough group because their literal survival depended on it. Once a week, for two years, I led a group named "Talk-it-Up." We ate pizza and talked about what was going in their world and possible coping strategies. In the beginning, those inner-city kids suspiciously tolerated me; they attended only for the free pizza. But eventually I won their trust. It was while I volunteered with the inner-city youth that my brother was killed in the plane crash and Nelly was murdered. I was committed to those kids, and I did not quit because of my grief. At the end of the school year, I was awarded "Volunteer of the Year" for the city of Atlanta. Doing this type of work convinced me that my heart was invested in being of service. I needed more education.

After this first round of cancer, I got more serious about my life. I returned to graduate school, this time choosing Pacifica Graduate Institute in Santa Barbara, California. I earned an MA in counseling with an emphasis in Jungian theory.

Each month for two years, I flew from Atlanta to Los Angeles and caught a commuter plane to Santa Barbara. When I arrived in Santa Barbara, I checked into a hotel and prepped for three very full days of intensive academics. For the return trip, I frequently boarded the infamous red-eye from LA to Atlanta. I returned home on Monday morning, sleep deprived, with academic assignments to complete and patients to see. Often, I arrived home just in time to awaken our son, make him breakfast, pack his lunch, and get him on the school bus. Finally, my dream to become a psychotherapist, and be of greater service, felt closer.

As I approached graduation, I was determined to not get derailed from completing my degree like I had when my brother's plane crashed. Death smiled, as if she knew something I didn't. Graduation was scheduled in four months; I had only to complete my thesis. *No problem*, I thought. It seemed like I was almost done. But then bomb number four arrived—and before its location and devastation is revealed, this story needs to go back in history.

Years before, I had befriended a woman named Debbie. I told her, "I know the perfect guy for you! The only problem is that he lives in Africa. I know long-distance relationships can be a challenge, but ..."

Debbie laughed. "No! I'm not interested in anyone. Are you crazy? Africa?"

I explained that Andy was dentist-turned-swashbuckling-safari-pilot in Kenya. This modern-day Romeo was a chick magnet that came complete with his own red biplane. I nagged Debbie for nearly two years to meet him.

I *knew* they were meant to be together. I was right—in retrospect, this event marks one of the first psychic events that took place in my life. Andy and Debbie finally met, and cupid's arrow hit them both—soulmates reunited. They married a year later. Life tasted sweet. Their sweet love created a little boy, and they moved to Idaho to raise him.

The morning of bomb number four, Andy was flying co-pilot. The captain turned the Cessna Citation from base to final. They were too fast. He said, "Jack, we're too hot!" Throttles pushed full forward to abort the landing and go around. Except the concrete embankment at the end of the runway seemed like it just wanted to hang on to that plane. The jet did not clear the concrete. The violence of the plane crash ejected him from the cockpit. As he lay in a ravine, fluid spewed everywhere. The fluid was aviation fuel. The fuel created a hungry fire. That hungry fire consumed everything. The legendary Andrew Garratt was dead.

Debbie and their son agonized in grief and despair. I was stricken with shock. When Debbie called to tell me of Andy's crash, I had just begun writing my thesis. The shock of Andy's death waylaid me but not completely; somehow, this time, I managed to work through my grief and graduate on schedule.

Our son matured, and our sweet, small family blossomed. I worked hard. For several years, I worked with the Department of Family and Child Services, providing therapy for children and their families to assist with reunification. I became a court-appointed therapist, which allowed me to make specific recommendations to the judge. While this work can be rewarding, clinician burnout is high. I listened to children who innocently described their incest or played it out on the floor in front of me. I heard the children describe in detail their parents' drug abuse or being thrown into one chaotic situation after another. When I finished with one family, the next dozen waited for their turn.

I gave it my all. One of my final times in court, the judge turned to me while I was seated in the witness box and stated, "Ms. Maiden, in all my years on the bench, I've never seen such a dedicated therapist who worked so hard on behalf of our children." I silently said to death, "See … look, I'm doing everything that we agreed—and more! Stop lurking in the shadows around me." But death didn't stop lurking, and soon thereafter, the fifth bomb arrived.

My cousin and her family had moved to a neighboring town. Her husband was a military attorney. We were happy to have them so close; family gatherings were made more special because of their presence. Her son, Graham, was wonderful about entertaining our younger son while adults gathered. Graham was a tall, handsome, creative young man. At twenty-two, he was scheduled to graduate from college soon. One night, while walking on a regular foot bridge, he slipped and fell 120 feet onto concrete. Graham was killed instantly. The toxicology report revealed that he was stone sober. Suicide was ruled out, but the details remain vague. My cousin, her husband, and Graham's sister never fully recovered. Life and death. Death and life. Neither seems to care if they create instant chaos.

Six months after Graham's death, I was diagnosed with cancer for a second time. Routine scans detected a small tumor on my upper thigh. More sarcoma. The cancer spread. Treatment protocol was simple: minor surgery. I felt fine. I was fine. Because God and I brokered a deal. We had a deal. And God would never not honor the deal. My optimism sustained me—and so did my denial. Life resumed to the previous familiar hum.

A happy family event brought many family members together. I was excited to see my dead brother's two sons again. Although we participated in their lives as schedules and travel permitted, it was complicated because we had all relocated to different states. Although our geographical paths split, we managed to get together for family reunions and celebrations. I had not seen the boys for several years—and when they entered the restaurant, my heart skipped. The boys were no longer the little boys my brother left behind. Although their father's death left lingering scars, they had grown into charming young men. That evening dinner revealed significant healing and growth; well-spoken and matured, my nephews were a joy. Rob's firstborn son, Douglas, and I remarked upon our identical hair.

After dinner, I coaxed Douglas to my bathroom to share my secret hair-care products. We stood in front of the bathroom mirror and marveled at our similarities. I demonstrated how Douglas could apply my secret hair-care products to harness his coarse curls. We laughed as I worked product through his hair. He really liked the result! This seemingly silly moment bonded us. The celebration ended, and everyone returned to their lives. Ever lurking, death hid in the shadows until it was time to knock on the door with bomb number six.

And this time, death literally knocked. Douglas opened the front door. He did not know that he opened it to his assassin. That assassin wanted money. Douglas did not easily yield. The penalty for not yielding was a bullet through his heart. His girlfriend held his head as he died. I understood sudden-death grief very well. But life needed to round out my spiritual resume.

As I processed the deaths of both Graham and Douglas, I continued my work as a psychotherapist at a prestigious practice. My patient caseload overflowed. I love being a therapist. And I'm good. But it's not because I'm smart. As my own therapist, Barry Williams, said, "Therapeutic brilliance never cures the patient. It's relatedness. It's love." I love my patients. I accept their psychological warts and wrinkles and love them all the same. My colleagues think I'm strange for enjoying my work with grievers, but I feel at home in it. No matter how diverse our experience of loss, death shakes us just the same.

For example, one patient's wife was killed in a car accident, while another patient lost her husband to cancer, and a teenaged patient lost his mother to encephalitis, while a mother inconsolably wept about her ten-year-old son's boating accident. I worked with children who grieved their parents or sibling, and parents who grieved their child or partner. The painful, raw reality of grief hits hard, and we often wept together. At the same time, I began to have mediumistic experiences—some of which I related to my eighty-four-year-old mother. I also frequently shared patient stories with her, carefully told to obscure the patient's identity. Her compassionate heart helped guide me.

My elderly parents lived a few miles from our home. I visited my mother nearly every Friday. She was undergoing regular dialysis for kidney disease. Her health suddenly plummeted, and I realized that her tether to life was fading. My cancer-screening scans were scheduled while she was in the hospital. I rescheduled the scans for a month later. One week before Christmas, my mother slipped across the veil. I do not consider my mother's death to be a bomb; she died of natural causes at an old age. Yet grief caught up with me just the same. Although I already understood that death is an illusion, I still cried and cried when my mother died. I loved her intensely.

January came to begin a new year: 2014. Emotionally, I felt sad regarding my mother's death, while physically, I felt great. But when I went in for a routine scan with my oncologist, the MRI revealed metastatic cancer. *M-E-T-A-S-T-A-T-I-C. Everywhere.*

It seems that this third time around, cancer is refusing to yield. As of this writing, I'm still in the storm. While cancerous tumors on my lungs, liver, bladder, and esophagus are currently stable, the tumor on the cardiac aortic node is naughty. It grew 50 percent in just four months. Recently, another tumor was identified on the tail of the pancreas. The hourglass of my life is running out. Slow but steady, drizzling sand passes through the portal and settles on the bottom. That visual compels me to write this story. The Spirit world is counting on me to complete my work.

A set of six bombs nearly blew up my sanity. They became my teachers, opening me to a compassion that flows on both sides of the veil. How can we hate the teacher because the lesson is hard? The culmination of these events led me to The Call—my sacred purpose.

I never made contact with my brother Rob. Similarly, I have not spoken to Nicole, Nelly, Andy, Graham, or Douglas—nor have I contacted my mother in the four years since she left. But these experiences opened me to the search. They gave me infinite compassion for others as they grieve, and this compassion is part of my drive to deliver the messages from the spirits I am able to contact. The story of how I learned to make this contact, and many other stories of these contact events, is told throughout the following pages.

Death brought me life. And life brought me the ability to see dead people, or spirits. Ironically, I don't see my own loved ones. I see yours. The following chapters are dedicated to all who have suffered agony and grief from the loss of their beloved.

This message is for you.

CHAPTER 2

First Contact

> Our bonds of love are never broken ... they cannot be broken ... Our bonds always continue ...
> —*Spirit*

His masculine scent swirled under my nose with a subtle-but-still-there combination of soap and sweat. It was heady. Why did he have to be so attractive? Jacques held the door open as I followed him into the small room, then firmly closed it behind us. I did not know then that this was a one-way ticket for spiritual growth. Once I crossed that threshold, it became impossible to exit as the same person. Mysterious forces stirred a cauldron of invisible energies. Those invisible energies were brewing a divine concoction. That divine brew would prove to be the metaphorical elixir that gave me the gift of sight—the gift of mediumship.

 I tried to imagine his muscular body doing something as dainty as fluffing delicate bed linens. But he must have. Everything was prepared. He was younger than I, so aloofness became my shield. I didn't want him to sense that he had any effect on me. What a foolish middle-aged woman was I to feel sexually attracted to a man who was twenty years my junior. When he instructed me to lie down, it sounded more like a command than an invitation. Silently, I obeyed. Small talk seemed silly. Our session began. Jacques was an excellent massage therapist. He skillfully manipulated my body as I yielded to his touch. Tension left me like steam evaporating from boiling water.

Everything magically aligned so this moment could occur in the fall of 2013. My mother's health seemed stable, my husband could be home with our teenaged son, and my work schedule cleared. I practice as a psychotherapist at a fantastic psychiatric practice. So, when my schedule miraculously cleared, it allowed me to attend a weeklong class on Spirit communications offered by internationally recognized medium James Van Praagh at the Omega Institute in Rhinebeck, New York. My excitement overflowed. This opportunity was a dream come true. I had voraciously read Van Praagh's books regarding his experiences with spirits and helping grievers heal. His work helped me survive the multiple shock losses I endured. I parsed out my expectations into two categories—minimum and maximum—and realized reality would probably fall somewhere in between.

At a minimum, I hoped someone there would provide me with evidential mediumship that my loved ones were still around me. The previous six bombs—the six sudden deaths of my loved ones—shattered me. Outwardly, I functioned, but in private moments, grief and sorrow sat by my side. Although my heart had mostly mended, it was still sore. I wanted evidence of life after death. I believed our loved ones reach across the veil and send us custom-made signs. But my skepticism still needed to see some proof. And I wanted relief from a neurotic pattern I had developed of calling mediums to connect with my loved ones. As I mentioned earlier, my behavior crossed into the neurotic zone when I couldn't stop it—and I felt the need to hide it from my husband. I already felt crazy—I didn't want him to see that I actually might be! A few psychic mediums we found were very helpful because they provided small, specific, evidential details that proved to both my mother and me that my brother was present. That style of deliver-the-evidence became my benchmark for all future mediums—a standard that was echoed by James Van Praagh himself.

At a maximum, I dared to hope to catch a glimpse of a real, live dead person! Specifically, I longed to make contact with the people I'd lost. If it only happened once, if I could see just one of them for a few seconds, then even one Spirit contact would be worth every dollar I spent to attend this workshop.

After the second day of class, I purchased a massage from the onsite spa. But as it turned out, I got much more than just a massage. My maximum expectations were exponentially exceeded.

Spirits appeared.

As I began to relax deeply, my scattered thoughts took flight and were replaced with quiet meditation. Exquisite colors pirouetted around and around behind my eyes. Cobalt blue and emerald green appeared. These colors pulsated with unearthly energy. It was as if they were plugged into an unseen divine electrical outlet. Glorious colors danced like prima ballerinas behind my closed eyes. Later, I would come to learn that this dance of colors that ends in cobalt blue serves as an angel's trumpet, announcing the parting of the veil. It indicates that Spirit is present and waiting to speak to me.

If I had known what was going to happen next, my body would have snapped shut like a Venus flytrap. I began to sense another woman in the room. I swear, I felt her watch us. She was there because she loved him. She wanted him to know of her continued love and frequent presence.

Some life moments beg to be consummated at an exact time. This was one of those moments. Before, the time is not yet the time, and after, the time is no longer the time. Timing is everything. The other woman calculated the exact moment to announce her presence. I heard her voice first. Then I saw her.

"That is my grandson! You have to tell him I am here."

What? Who said that? Silence.

Minutes passed, but the woman remained. I knew she was there because I felt her presence. My body must have stiffened because Jacques asked if I was okay. I nodded. He continued, and I realized he did not know the other woman was in the room. Again, she spoke. Firmly, she ordered me to "Tell him! Tell him that I am here. I am his grandmother. I helped raise him. See my crooked fingers? They are all bent from arthritis. See?"

I still did not believe what I heard. I was tired. This was my imagination. Weird though, she even had an accent. I hoped the previous relaxed state would return and this voice inside of my head would stop. Jacques worked his knowing hands up from my feet to my legs. I liked his touch.

The woman started to talk again. I silently shouted, "Shut up!" I had booked the massage before I arrived at the conference—and it was expensive. I didn't want to hear the chatter of some woman that I did not know about, care about, or even necessarily believe was real. I needed body work. I needed to relax. Where was she anyway? It all seemed so confusing. She started to talk again. *Oh God, no!* This time, I saw images with her narrative. At first, it was like looking at an old photo album or a still photograph. For example, when she said that she had sometimes smoked cigarettes, I saw her image holding a cigarette.

Suddenly, the images began to appear in rapid succession. It was as if somebody turned pages of a photo album faster and faster until it became a slide show. The slide show shifted to a movie, and important aspects of her life played out in my head. I saw her petite figure and gray hair pulled back in a bun. I saw her holding an old-fashioned, primitive-type wooden paddle—the kind my elementary school teacher hung in the classroom to ensure students obeyed. She said, "Sometimes I had to use this—to make sure he was a good boy. But now, I think, I was too harsh." When she realized that I could hear her and see everything she showed me, she triumphantly ordered: "Now you tell him!"

Irreverently, I silently responded, "I don't believe you're real, so I'm not saying a word! Besides, he would think I am crazy—and I wouldn't blame him. Then it would be all awkward. We'd be stuck in here together for the next, what, forty-five minutes? No way! I'm not doing it. So whoever and whatever you are, you need to go."

The old woman just smiled at me. She smiled in a way that made me uncomfortable. She crossed her arms over her full bosom and replied in broken English, "Okay, I wait. Then you tell him that I am here." I thought, *This must be the definition of insanity—arguing with a dead person. Wait until I tell my colleagues at the psychiatric practice about this—or maybe I won't ...*

I thought perhaps humor would make the voice stop. Maybe she'd disappear. I telepathically communicated, "Hey this is my massage, so don't butt in on my time! Who's paying for this anyway? The answer is: me!" For the first time, I became aware of the strength of a Spirit's determination to deliver a message to their loved one. Her patience and perseverance were simultaneously impressive and unnerving. She did not budge. Defiantly, the old woman remained.

She showed me more images. I saw her silver hair pulled into a bun off of her face. Her deeply lined face did not diminish her beauty. Her fierce Spirit felt disproportionate to her petite frame. She showed me herself standing in front of a humble home. I actually felt her energy, her personality. She was not in any way mean, hostile, or threatening. Just spirited.

Hours earlier, I prayed to be given the ability of mediumship. I struggled to believe that I could actually ever have this ability. I ached to see spirits because I wanted to make contact with all of the people I loved who died. I wanted to see my deceased loved ones with my own eyes—because then I would know, *really know*, that death is an illusion. This woman, this supposed Spirit, provided more than the minimum of four pieces of evidence that James Van Praagh had taught us to receive earlier that day.

What if she was real? I knew that I had strong psychic ability, but mediumship is an entirely different ball field. I'd learned in the workshop that though all mediums are psychic, not every psychic is a medium. My panic swelled like hot air filling a balloon. I was about to burst with so many conflicted feelings. If I told Jacques what I had seen, and if he didn't have a grandmother that matched my description, I would look crazy. And if I looked crazy, I would not only have to make it through the rest of the massage but actually dodge from this guy the rest of the week due to my extreme embarrassment.

But what if I did not speak? What if I didn't speak my truth? Then I might walk away and wonder if it was truly my first Spirit contact. *What if I miss it? But this is so easy! How could it be this easy!* Listening to the old woman Spirit talk and show images was as simple as turning on the television. *What if I am her only opportunity to relay a message to her beloved grandson? What if I squandered a divine gift?*

What if I have been arguing with a real Spirit? Is that possible?

With all of these conflicting thoughts whirling in my head, I could not focus on my massage. What if I was the conduit to facilitate healing for them both? I remembered all of the loved ones I had lost to death. I remembered the gut-wrenching longing to be reassured of their continued existence. Thousands of thoughts galloped like racehorses through my mind. I know what it is like to be held hostage by grief. Grief can render the person left behind a big, neurotic puddle of dysfunctional despair.

Then I remembered something a classmate said earlier that day: "If Spirit gives you a message, you are obliged to deliver it." Ugggghhhhhhhh. That was the tipping point when I knew I must speak.

I took a deep breath for courage. I opened my eyes and sheepishly said, "Uh, Jacques? Ummm, uh, could you stop for a minute?" He looked at me with question marks for eyes. I propped myself up on my elbows and hesitantly said, "I know this is going to be a strange question, but do you have a grandmother who has crossed over? Uh, well, you know, passed over—as in, died?"

He said, "Yes."

His guarded expression suggested that he had no idea where I was going with this question. I added, "When you were young, did you live with her sometimes? Did she help raise you?"

Jacques responded, "Uh, yeah."

I blurted, "She's here! Your grandmother is here in this room. And she won't leave me alone until I deliver a message. She wants you to know that she loves you! She is so proud of you!" Then I quickly gave him some context about the workshop and James Van Praagh and my absolute inexperience with communicating across the veil. When I finished stumbling over my words and apologizing for myself, Jacques's silence spoke volumes.

He looked hard into my eyes like an investigator evaluating a suspect as he tried to assess the veracity of my story. He didn't know what to say. The dreaded awkward moment hung in the space between us.

Jacques's grandmother appeared again, as if she did not want this opportunity to pass without proving her presence to her grandson. Rapidly, she showed me more evidence. I telepathically asked her how she died, and she showed me her chest and heart area. I struggled to understand what caused her death. I could not discern whether or not she died from pneumonia or heart attack. Then I heard the words "congestive heart failure." Once I grasped a piece of information, she moved on to show me another.

Over and over again, she repeated her name. This seemed to be an important piece of evidence. I heard "MMMMeeeeee" sound. She said "et" over and over. She told me, "I have many grandchildren, but he's my favorite! He was always my favorite grandson. I am so proud of him! I am surprised that he chose this career. I used to call him 'my little favorite.' He knows this. You tell him now." I relayed everything she shared. And I emphasized what she told me about her nickname for him.

Jacques's facial response affirmed the accuracy of the evidence I had shared. "Wow!" he exclaimed. "Wow … oh my God! This is so weird! She used to call me 'Mon petit préféré,' which in French means, 'My little favorite.'" Jacques confirmed every detail, even her name: Marie Ruet. As her nickname for him was in French, I had an opportunity to see for the first time that Spirit communicates telepathically—not through literal language. The medium and Spirit do not have to know the same language, because Spirit's knowledge goes far beyond language; Spirit expresses itself however it thinks the medium will be able to comprehend.

Minutes before, he questioned. Now, he believed. Goose bumps and tears were my physical affirmation. It was the first time I ever had a Spirit contact. Or at least, this was the first time that I had evidence and someone else to verify it. He believed that his grandmother was in that room. Jacques's belief helped me believe too.

I lay back down. Jacques resumed my massage. Although his grandmother was still in the room with us, she was not in the forefront anymore. I tried to relax. My mind whirled like a spinning top. How could anyone feel calm after talking to a dead person? Even though Jacques confirmed every piece of evidence his grandmother provided, doubt crept in.

Maybe I was just a really good guesser. Everybody has a grandmother, and probably half of people over a certain age have a deceased grandmother. Marie is a common name, and M an even more common first initial. Most Europeans of that generation smoked cigarettes. And what old person doesn't exhibit some arthritic deformity in their fingers? Doubt grew. Suddenly this event did not sound special at all. The shock and awe I felt moments earlier faded as I discredited my experience. Emotionally, I imagine I felt like a rapid-cycling bipolar patient— from exhilaration to depression in minutes. But then something happened. Well, really, some*one* happened. He arrived.

As the massage continued, a man entered into my awareness.

First, I saw him. I imagined he could have been a finalist in the contest for the world's most handsome man, or maybe been on the cover of *Conde Nast* travel magazine. Probably both. In my mind, I saw sun-bleached blond hair that suggested he'd just gotten off his sailboat. His tanned skin covered a sculpted jawline. He was tall. He was slender. He was athletic. His physique was a tailor's dream. The custom silk suits he wore helped complete his debonair persona—which increased his tailor's financial success too. He showed me that he was around thirty-five or forty years old when he transitioned. Within minutes, I literally saw all of these facts.

Second, I felt his energy. His energy was softer than his silk suits. This man showed me that though he had to wear a tough façade in his line of work, he was able to be emotionally vulnerable with the people he loved.

Wait! What was happening? Why was this new image coming to me? My left, rational brain began to rule out all of the possibilities. Maybe I was having a psychotic break. Maybe this guy was an anxiety-induced hallucination. As a psychotherapist, this sort of rapid categorization is what I do with patients. The patient's constellation of symptoms often suggest many possible diagnoses, so I list them internally and then rule out the possibilities. For one thing, I was sure I had never met this man before, and so it could not be a memory. Right?

Third, he spoke—I *heard* him speak. No way. This could not be happening again. The handsome blond man in my vision was so loving and patient with me. As I tried to deny his existence, he gently continued to telepathically show me important specific details of his life and his relationship with the man massaging me.

He pointed to Jacques and said, "I love him like a brother. Please tell him that I am here. Please tell him how much I love him."

Before I could garner more courage to say anything to Jacques, I had some questions for this blond man. Voiceless, I asked, "Who are you?"

The blond man said, "We are like brothers; our love was so strong. Our bond can never be broken. We were so close, like brothers ... we were like this ..." Then the blond man showed me a gesture where he tapped both his forefinger and middle fingers of both hands together over and over again. I was not quite sure what this meant; however, it appeared to indicate a strong emotional bond.

I decided to play along and pretend that the blond man was real. So I asked, "How did you die? What happened?" His answer played in my mind just like a movie on a screen. I saw him dressed in one of the silk suits he showed me earlier. He confidently walked on a crowded city sidewalk at night. He was going to meet someone. A casually dressed stranger approached him. Before the blond man knew what was happening, the stranger jammed a gun barrel into his chest. One bullet discharged. He fell to the sidewalk. People stepped back, not knowing what to do. It was no accident. It was some kind of preordained, well-thought-out assassination. He was killed because of his line of work, which he indicated was very risky business.

Over and over again, the blond man showed me that he was shot directly in his chest. This detail seemed very important to him. He played his death scene many times to ensure I understood. I needed to confirm what I saw. "So you were not shot in the back, or head, or stomach, right?"

He said, "That is correct. I was shot right here [he pointed to his chest], only one bullet. I was so surprised, so surprised. I had no idea what happened. I transitioned very quickly."

The blond man allowed me to rest for a few seconds so that I could grasp everything he told me. Then, I said, "Okay, I think I get it. Can you please tell me your name ... what was your name?"

I heard him respond, "My name was ffffffff, eeeeeeee ..."

I guessed, "Uhhh, you mean Frank, or Fred?"

The blond man patiently repeated, "No ... fffffeeyyyy ... Please tell him, tell him that I am here and that I love him. We were like brothers."

Conflicted feelings wrestled in my mind like two martial art masters. One master said, *This is not real.* The other master said, *Spirit is here. What are you going to do?* I had asked—begged—for the gift of seeing spirits, and now that my wish had been granted, I had trouble believing it. While I reasoned that I could have conjured everything about the grandmother's appearance in my mind alone, there was no way I could guess the details that the blond man provided me.

I felt like I was about to dive off of a very high cliff. I raised my arms and dove.

Opening my eyes, I stammered, "Uh, Jacques, um, you're not gonna believe this, and I know this is so weird—I'm sorry, but it seems like someone else is here ..." Jacques stopped moving his hands and looked at me. I reiterated, "Maybe this is completely my imagination ... but now a man is here." Jacques waited while I told him what I saw, heard, and felt in exact detail. This time, painful memories moved across his face. In speechless disbelief, Jacques stared at me. I gently asked, "Does any of this make sense to you?" Jacques nodded.

The blond man was his stepfather. They had been extremely close. And his name? His name was Phillippe. Jacques quietly added that the city I saw was Paris. Lastly, Jacques added something to this story that I did not know. Jacques confided that it was impossible for me to know all of this. Why? Because nobody in his family even knew the truth of what happened. Nobody knew that the blond man named Phillippe was assassinated—except Jacques and his mother. Other family members were told that Phillippe had a congenital heart issue that led to a fatal cardiac arrest, because the circumstances around his death involved a line of work he had kept secret.

As Jacques received the evidence Phillippe provided, I felt triumphant. *I just had my first verifiable contact with Spirit!*

After the massage, I returned to my hotel room and replayed the events again and again in my mind. How could I think of anything else? This was the most mind-blowing experience of my life. But I wanted to be correct in my conclusion: that I saw spirits. I therefore tried to find any other plausible explanation for what I saw, what I heard, what I felt, and what I *knew*. Inner doubt stalked me like a hunter trails its prey.

It was easier to accept any reality other than the one wherein I talked to dead people. But a complete stranger verified every detail. In fact, not only had Jacques verified the specifics I presented, he was emotionally pulled toward my description. At this point, I still felt hesitant to express an inner hallelujah. But no other explanation fit. I really did talk to Spirit.

I tried to sleep. But sleep had wings that night, and it flew away. Now that I had actually had that experience, I had so many questions to ask James Van Praagh the following day. I catalogued those questions in my mind. I wanted to know why Spirit only appeared on my right side; whether it was normal to hear specific accents; how Spirit shows the scene of death over and over; whether they all continue with such unique personalities like they did when they lived in a body; why I heard single syllables instead of entire names; whether I'd handled the contacts well; whether I was going to get a gold star for being a special student. Questions bounced back and forth like Ping-Pong balls.

Finally, out of my internal chaos, I heard a voice say, "Our bonds of love are never broken ... they cannot be broken. Our bonds always continue—always." It was Spirit. That voice settled me. Sleep returned. When I awakened the next morning, I arrived at class early to share my first experience with my teacher—someone who I knew would believe me.

When James Van Praagh entered, I ran to him. I felt breathless as I blurted out the details of what had happened twelve hours earlier.

James nodded. He listened. He did not seem nearly as excited as I was. He crossed his arms over his beefy chest. He told me that he realized I was excited and he believed me. But he chastised me as he reminded me that mediums cannot be in the world and always open to spirits showing up. I cringed at his light reprimand. My elation fell to deflation.

I understand now that James was right. His concern was valid. I hadn't invited this contact; I'd intended to just receive a massage. He knew that an open-door policy with Spirit can actually drive people mad. Spirit is eager to comfort the grieving loved ones they left behind, and a receptive medium catches their attention like a neon sign. Spirit must adhere to the medium's rules, but if the medium does not have any rules—as I did not yet—then the door is left wide open. Spirit will walk through that door, crossing the veil to send a message of comfort to their loved one.

Spirits are shameless opportunists; just knowing that should provide every griever with comfort. Loved ones who have crossed over will do almost anything to give us a sign and send a message. Though they are diverse in their methods, they are fueled by the same energy: love.

I was embarrassed and confused to receive his admonishment. I knew I had a lot to learn. Yet I left the workshop with a sense of hope I hadn't felt in years. I had made contact. I had successfully communicated with Spirit.

That first experience of bridging the world of the physical and the world of Spirit took place over four years ago. I did not know then that several years later, I would actually straddle these two worlds—because these worlds are intimately intertwined. Life and death are different sides of the same coin. They reside together.

Spirit continues to show me that there is no such thing as death. Again and again, it reminds me that death is an illusion—and all the while, cancer keeps calling my name.

CHAPTER 3

Diagnosis: Terminal Cancer

You don't have to die to have access to this world.
—*Spirit*

Zzzzzsssssssiiisssst. Tttssszzzziizzssst. *Torture. Tight. Tube. Coffin? Claustrophobia. What? Where Am I? Panic.* Zzzzsssissst. Zzzzist. Buzzzzzzzzz. Fire said, "Hisssssszzzz … pop-pop-sizzle-crack! As you burn, you can't turn back." Freshly burned flesh filled my nose. The stench so sickened me that vomit waited to exit my mouth. But vomit and I were stuck. There was no way for either of us to exit.

Indescribable pain.

I had signed the consent form for this medical procedure that utilizes a powerful laser on the end of a long, flexible tube. A surgeon makes a small incision and inserts the tube into the patient. Then the patient is tightly strapped with medical Velcro to the gurney in a CAT scan machine. This technique allows the surgeon to locate tumors and burn them with the laser. I was supposed to be sedated, and a nurse was assigned to monitor me during the entire procedure. The sedation wore off, and the nurse decided it was more interesting to watch the attractive surgeon perform a new procedure than to watch an unconscious patient—although she did place an emergency call button in my hand, "Just in case you need us ..." So, what could possibly go wrong?

What went wrong? I woke up. In the middle of an excruciating surgical procedure to burn tumors from the inside out, I woke up. But because they did not properly monitor me, nobody knew.

The surgeon was in another room with the robot-laser device. The monitoring nurse was too. "Hello?" I whispered. "Is anyone there? *Please.* Hello? Can you guys hear me? *Stop!* Please stop this! I am awake! I can feel everything!" I tried to speak louder. I couldn't. A recent surgery on my liver—also aimed at removing tumors—made it impossible to inhale a full breath. I could not scream. My voice reached nowhere and to no one. The emergency call button had fallen out of my hand. It teased me from just out of reach. Because my entire body and head and neck were medically tied down, I had zero capacity for movement.

Zzzzzsssssssiiitttttt. Searing heat torched another tumor. Fire said, "Burn baby burn ... like the disco inferno ..." and I did. I started to cry. Then I realized that if cried, I would be unable to breathe; I would choke on tears and mucous. I stopped. I prayed. I pleaded with God and my guides and angels and every compassionate entity in the universe. *Please, please, please release me.* Zzzsssssssiiiiittttttt. More burning.

Either from pain or prayers, I passed out. I don't know how much time elapsed before the surgeon rolled the gurney out of the CAT scan machine. He rubbed my head and innocently asked, "Hi, Mrs. Maiden, how are you doing? We're nearly halfway done with the procedure. Are you okay?"

I started to sob. "No! I woke up! I felt you burning my flesh! I smelled it! I heard my flesh crackling just like eggs on a hot skillet! I tried to scream, but I couldn't! I thought there was supposed to be a camera in the CAT scan machine! The call button fell out of my hand!"

He nodded nervously; my description of events was too accurate. He believed me. He apologized. He mumbled for the nurse to increase the IV sedation medications so I could endure the next round of tumor burning.

The next time I awakened, I was in the recovery room. I have been taught that the human brain is incapable of remembering physical pain, and perhaps it truly is. But I do remember the emotional torture as a result from what was physically done to me. This is the drama and trauma of cancer treatment.

A few weeks earlier, I felt fine. Since I had been cancer-free for five years, I was able to reapply for life insurance. I completed the paperwork and sent it in. "Not so fast," death whispered again.

I went in for my annual cancer scans. I felt slightly annoyed to cancel a full day of my patient caseload. I wore crème corduroy pants and a gray, beaded cardigan sweater. I looked healthy. My oncologist entered the room. I anticipated he would tell me everything looked good, exchange typical pleasantries, and end our appointment with the usual, "You look great! See you in a year." I sat on the end of the exam table and smiled as he entered the room. Instead of his normal bear hug, he hurriedly closed the door and looked at me. He got right to the point. And you know what happened next, because I already told you. It's the details I have yet to reveal.

"Suzanne, what the hell happened to your immune system? You're raining tumors. You've got tumors everywhere; they're all over the place! The radiologist is still texting me as he finds more from your scans today!" As the oncologist said this, it felt much more accusatory than empathetic. The cancer called sarcoma had returned. But this time it was metastatic, meaning the cancer had spread to other parts of my body—and was still spreading.

In the weeks, months, and ultimately years that followed that appointment, my body became a metaphorical battlefield, complete with blood shed, chemical warfare, and nuclear radiation. Multiple surgeries, six months of chemotherapy, radiation to three different tumor sites, and an entire year of Interferon injections wore me down. I felt broken, isolated, and depleted. And Spirit kept showing up. Life felt like one big setup.

In that initial phase of acute treatment, I had hours and days of alone time to rest and reflect and recover. And, of course, I was still grieving my mother, whom I had lost just a few months prior to my diagnosis. I lost myself in meditation. During one of those quiet moments, I remembered the stories of spiritual experiences that my mother and her sister used to share with me.

As a young child, I listened to my mother and her sister whisper and giggle about their secret life of seeing spirits and gathering information regarding other people through psychic means. Both my mother and my aunt were wives of prominent men. They kept their abilities to themselves and instead used them on their children and husbands. As a result, I seldom got away with anything. My mother just *knew* stuff. It was uncanny. My mother and her sister were the most spiritual, soulful, giving, kindhearted women I have ever known. Both of them exemplified compassion in action. Their faith in God was unshakeable. I owe them deep gratitude.

Although I already told you how my mother died, I did not tell you her last psychic prediction. The nineteenth of December was both my mother's birthdate and the date of her death. Several weeks before she died, she worked in the kitchen and prepared dinner. In a nonchalant manner, she said, "I am going to die on my birthday." Although she was in dialysis for kidney disease, she seemed like she was doing fairly well—but my mother's psychic predictions were as solid as gold coins in a safety deposit box.

As my mother's kidney disease progressed, I spent more time with her. We snuggled, and I shared current Spirit contact stories. Everything was new for me and very exciting—yet there were few people with whom to share it. There were few people I knew would believe me. My mother was one of them. She said, "Honey, this is so beautiful. You're taking your skills way past what I can do, and you will help so many people! I'm so proud of you, sweetheart." On her eighty-fifth birthday, my mother quietly took her last breath as her family sat around her. My mother and I were very close, which meant sometimes it was good and sometimes we disagreed. I loved her intensely.

A lot happened within a four-week period. First, my mother died. Second, we held her memorial service. Third, I made an expensive investment and purchased a historical home to begin an alternative healing facility, where I also moved part of my psychotherapy practice. Fourth, I was diagnosed with metastatic cancer.

The earth continued to spin—and so did I. Somehow, everything happened in slow motion *and* at warp speed. I felt as if I were drowning in both life and death. Where was a life preserver? As if to comfort and reassure me, unbidden, Spirit continued to appear. Doubt, skepticism, and fear held my voice hostage. But Spirit refused to be held captive. I hated cancer. But how can I hate the very thing that brought me my life? Without cancer, I wouldn't be alive. Not really. Because by threatening to kill me, cancer shoved me onto my knees—just as death had done when it took the people I loved. When I was on my knees, I prayed without ceasing—a process that stripped away some of my ego and my vanity. Humility became my friend.

Only when I lost myself did I find God. Hours alone in stillness and silence opened the portal so that I could see Spirit more clearly. Maybe others don't have to walk through the proverbial fire to access the divine. I did. Could I have learned how to communicate with Spirit without all of the trauma-drama? Maybe. Everyone's journey is unique.

As I went deeper into my mediumship, I noticed that despite the unique personalities and details Spirit provides, the message is basically the same. All of your loved ones across the veil want you to know the same set of things: They are not dead. Death is an illusion. They love you. They are still around you. They are aware of significant events in your life. They send you signs of their existence. And they are cheering you on, every moment of your life, until you return home, across the veil, where they will be waiting for you.

As cancer continued to consume me, Spirits increased their visits. I am not afraid of death, but I am terrified of suffering. It was as if Spirit appeared for two reasons: to communicate with a loved one through a willing messenger, and to provide some comfort for the messenger herself.

Spirits appeared while I spoke with complete strangers—many of whom I met in the hospital for treatment. During one round of chemotherapy, I experienced shortness of breath—a possible side effect from that particular chemo and one that can indicate heart damage. Treatment was suspended until my heart was evaluated by a cardiologist. For the most part, my husband hides his anxiety well. But when he chews his fingernails like a piece of beef jerky, I know his stress meter is pegged. He patiently drove an hour and a half for us to consult with a cardiac surgeon whom we had never met, seen, or heard of before then.

How could I have known that this cardiologist's deceased grandfather was waiting for our arrival?

Dr. Amore counseled another patient in the adjacent room. I was the last patient for the day. I lay on the exam table and meditated to manage my anxiety. My emotionally and physically exhausted husband fell asleep in the chair behind me. I heard his even breathing and light snores. As my meditation deepened, intense, indescribable colors erupted like fireworks behind my closed eyes. Saturated colors gushed with glorious God energy. Our language fails to convey the holiness of such moments. I knew Spirit was present. I knew Spirit was waiting to speak.

A grandfather energy appeared in Spirit. For me, Spirit appears in my mind's eye. I can hear them speak—especially if they want me to hear an accent from their country of origin; I see images flash over and over again; I smell scents associated with them;

and I feel literal physical pain related to pain they experienced when they lived in a body. The sum of this data provides accurate, descriptive, no-way-I-could-have-guessed-that-one evidence for their loved one.

In a heavy accent, Spirit said, "That is my grandson in the next room. Please tell him I love him and am so proud of him!" Although he told me his name, it was too complicated for me to understand and for my tongue to replicate. Why? Because some names, especially foreign-sounding and unfamiliar, are difficult to understand. In general, I'm much better at getting names—I mean like I have been dead-on accurate in name confirmation, as you will see in the following chapters. However, when Spirit gives me a foreign name—with multiple syllables—I get lost fairly fast. I can repeat what I hear phonetically, which is enough for most people.

Spirit continued, "I immigrated to this country when I was young, very young, from Eastern Europe." I saw that he was short and had big ears. I felt immense kindness emanate from him. While alive in his body, he was a humanitarian, tenderhearted toward the trials and tribulations of others. Spirit said, "I am his paternal grandfather, although our last names differ. I worked with my hands." He showed me this; small metal pieces flashed through my mind.

I asked, "Were you a watchmaker?"

He flashed another picture, this time with a sewing machine—aha! The metal I saw was a sewing needle! Then I saw him feeding fabric into a sewing machine. Spirit said, "My grandson completed my unlived dream: I wanted to be a surgeon. Please tell him how proud I am of him, and I am around him all of the time."

Dr. Amore entered. He said my heart was perfect and very healthy. He asked me if I had any questions for him. Now was the awkward moment. I asked if I could share something. I forewarned him that it had nothing to do with cardiology. He gently encouraged me to continue. Trepidation and fear stuck to me like feathers on tar.

There, with my long, skinny legs dangling off the table, I inhaled courage. My eyes locked with Dr. Amore's, and I asked if his grandfather immigrated to this country. He nodded. I asked, "Did he do fine work with his hands?"

The doctor said, "Yes, he was a tailor in a sweatshop in NYC. He emigrated from Eastern Europe to escape religious persecution." I shared everything his grandfather showed me. Dr. Amore got very emotional and choked up. He took a step back—a step away from me. Literally. After several years, I have come to recognize that when someone physically steps back, it is because their belief steps up—they realize something sacred is unfolding. At the time, though, I was somewhat surprised by such a physical reaction. He excitedly told me he had been working on an ancestry book and thought about his grandfather often. Then, his direction darted to my husband, as if he was silently seeking confirmation that I was stable.

Robin, who has become rather used to these looks, said, "My wife has a gift. Listen."

Dr. Amore confirmed everything I had seen. I asked Dr. Amore for clarification as to why his last name was different from that of his paternal grandfather. Dr. Amore explained that when his paternal grandfather immigrated through Staten Island, New York, the immigration officer could not pronounce his name, so the officer officially changed the name to something simpler.

Our time ended. Dr. Amore reached out and took my right hand. He bowed slightly as he tenderly kissed the back of my hand, saying, "In all of my years, I have never had this happen. What a gift you have given to me. Thank you."

Incidents like this continued to take place. Since so much of my time was spent in medical treatment, and since I was exposed to new people all the time through this treatment, Spirit often showed up at or around my appointments. Another time,

I was in the CAT scan machine. As the tech prepped me, her grandfather appeared. The grandfather showed me his tribal tunic with specific colors. He carried an assault rifle and had a band of men under his lead. Their country was in civil war. He showed me a significant battle scar above his left eye. He wanted his granddaughter to know that he had made a huge mistake. He spent his entire life trying to figure out how to kill people while she was in the profession of trying to help people heal. He had so much remorse for what he felt was a wasted opportunity on Earth. I shared his message with the tech, and she confirmed everything. She was so spooked, though, that she never returned! This is the downside of sharing what I see. Experiences like this one taught me that just because I can see Spirit does not mean everyone is ready to hear about it—or even wants to know. Some people grip tightly to their religious beliefs regarding Spirit contact; they consider it "evil" or "the work of the devil." I have learned to use cautious discernment.

Another time, Spirit made a surprise guest appearance while a nurse I knew quite well accessed my port for a blood draw. As I sat in the chair, Hope prepped me for the procedure. She chatted and worked. She told me she felt sad because her father had died. I asked her, "How did your father die?"

But before she could answer, her father did! "Heart attack." Like it usually does, the voice came from my right—and sure enough, Hope's father appeared there. Or, at least, he appeared to me.

Then Hope said, "It was a heart attack." Then her father showed me how he started to roll his own cigarettes as a young boy, around the age of ten, while he bounced on the back of a tractor. He grew up on a farm.

All the while, Hope was trying to access my port. That means she was physically probing the port "bump" to assess where to punch the needle in. That needle is the diameter of a thumbtack. It's big, and it hurts. As part of the medical protocol, both the nurse and I must wear surgical masks to create a sterile field, because the port is connected to a cardiac artery.

A host of sensations occurred simultaneously. The nurse poked and prodded me while, unbeknownst to her, her dead father-in-Spirit talked to me. I was listening to my body, listening to Spirit, and trying to figure out whether I should even deliver the message—whether Hope was ready to hear it. I understand now why my Spirit communications teachers strongly encourage people who work as mediums to define clear boundaries for the Spirit world. It's really challenging to have so many things happening at the same time! At the time, I was still learning how to define and hold those boundaries.

I casually noted that her father had smoked cigarettes. She kept working on my port and casually said, "Yeah, he did. He smoked his whole life. Wait, how did you know that?"

I said, "Um, because, well, uh, he's right here. And he is showing me that he began to roll his own cigarettes as a young boy while he bounced on the back of a tractor."

There in the examination room, Hope began to emotionally unravel. Her tears flowed like torrential rain. Her hands shook. She lost her focus. And her father provided me with more evidence. For example, Spirit said, "Her mama one difficult woman. She was a real hell cat!"

The nurse said, "Oh my God! He used to say my mama was hell-on-heels!" Although I did not get the verbiage exactly correct, she accepted it as close enough. Because she was so shocked, she jumped back away from me, and my port paraphernalia was left dangling in the air.

Later, as I waited in the lobby to check out, I overheard one of the schedulers ask where Hope had gone. Another answered, "I don't know what happened to her, but she's in the bathroom crying."

I've seen Hope many times now. We hug each time we meet. She profusely thanks me because I connected her to her beloved father. Though the first time I told her about it she was deeply rattled, she understands that the messages he sends are real, and she cherishes them. For reasons I do not understand, her father has appeared several more times when she is around me. Each time, he provides detailed facts.

I saw Hope again recently. This time, her father popped up to show me how he used to suck on lemons. He had a huge lemon wedge in between his smiling lips—I thought I was hallucinating! I asked Hope, "Did your father suck on lemons?"

Once again, she lost her junk. She threw up her arms and loudly exclaimed, "Lordy, Lordy, Ms. Suzanne! Yes! Is he here? Oh my God! In the summertime, he used to make us kids homemade lemonade. When we finished the pitcher, he retrieved the lemons and told us they were too full of nutrients to throw out. So he sucked on them! And he would tease us kids with a big old lemon wedge in between his lips." I'm not clever enough to make this stuff up. It's true. I cannot explain how or why it happens.

And it keeps happening. Several months after my first experience with Hope and her dead father, I was at the hospital again for blood work. Apparently, word of my ability had spread amongst the staff.

As I waited in the checkout line at the hematologist's office, I felt someone staring at me. I turned and saw a dark-skinned, heavyset woman. Our eyes met. She stood with several other hospital staff. She sized me up. Her arms crossed over her full figure, dressed in surgical scrubs. After she gave me the once-over, she walked toward me. Unsmiling, she firmly stated, "I hear you got a gift." Her words sounded more like a challenge than a question. She was quite intimidating.

I hesitated. I knew what she meant, but I still felt unsure of my abilities. I also felt tired after a long day at the hospital. My husband and father waited for me. They too were tired.

And Atlanta traffic would be a nightmare this time of day. My resistance surfaced. But I heard myself say, "Yes."

She looked down the hall, as if to scout out a location. Then, without emotion, she asked, "Can I talk to you for a minute—over there?"

I followed her into a small room, and she pulled the curtain behind us. I noticed that her name tag said *Shannequa*. She said, "I lost a brother, and I just want to know if he's okay ... I mean, like, is he in heaven?" Immediately, her dead brother appeared in Spirit and stood on my right side. He gave me the rapid download of information about his life—some of it telepathic, some with his voice, and a good deal via slide show. Spirit will use any combination of ways to communicate. They will try every way—and any way—to get their story across with as much accuracy as possible for the medium.

I heard Spirit say, "I was shot right here ..." Then he showed me his abdominal area. I repeated his words and image to his sister. Her previous flat effect morphed into an emotional avalanche. She literally doubled over in tears and collapsed onto me. Guttural groans escaped her mouth. My heart ached as I witnessed her agony.

Spirit indicated he could not stay long. He had to tell his sister something quickly. He said, "Ask her about JJJJJjjjjjjaaaaaa ... tell her this name ... jjjjjeeeeeaaaaa."

I said, "Who is someone whose name begins with a Ja sound? Maybe James? Why is your brother so insistent on telling me this name? Was it his name?"

More tears streaked down her face as she answered, "No. Oh my God! It's my son. I have a son, named Germaine. I just sent him back to Chicago to live with his daddy, but I'm really worried about him."

Spirit said, "Tell her that I am watching him and nudging him to make different life choices than I did. I agreed to stay back to help him as part of my spiritual growth because of the way I led my life. I am with him … to help, to be of service. I guide [him]. I am one of his Spirit guides now." Shannequa sobbed with rel[ief]. She seemed comforted to know that her son was being divinely watched and that her brother still played an integral role in their family.

She felt relief because her brother's message allowed her to zoom out and see his death in the greater context of their family's journey together. I suppose these messages do the same thing for me as I continue to undergo the poking and prodding, the testing and treating—and, occasionally, the flesh-searing burning—that comes along with cancer. I still don't fully understand the role my diagnosis plays in relation to my gift, but receiving the two in such quick succession provides an interesting context for my own journey here.

I continue to walk through the world with cancer. I never know when it might suddenly sever the connection between my Spirit and my body. I do know this, because I've heard it again and again: love cannot be severed. Love's invincible force binds us together forever and always.

CHAPTER 4

The Naked Medium

> The most beautiful and most profound experience is the sensation of the mystical. It is the sower of all true science. He to whom this emotion is a stranger, who can no longer wonder and stand rapt in awe, is as good as dead. To know that what is impenetrable to us really exists, manifesting itself as the highest wisdom and the most radiant beauty which our dull faculties can comprehend only in their primitive forms—this knowledge, this feeling is at the center of true religiousness.
>
> —*Albert Einstein, The Merging of Spirit and Science*

Sticky ammonia, salt, and sugars formed pearl-sized drops that ran like melted ice cream beneath my breasts. Human sweat. In tandem, perspiration slid down both sides in a race for my waistline. The bathroom air, saturated with moisture, teased my naturally curly, coarse hair to mimic Medusa. Even expensive anti-frizz hair products were no defense for southern humidity.

Not wanting to risk sweating even more, I grabbed my blow-dryer and began the process of preparing for my day. I decided to remain naked to cool off more quickly. I thought I was alone. I wasn't.

I was fortunate to receive excellent instruction from respected teachers in the early days of my journey with mediumship—and these studies continue, to the extent that I can schedule them in tandem with cancer treatments and a professional caseload. While I heard everything that was said in those early seminars and courses, putting it all into practice proved to be a real challenge at the beginning. As a new medium, I made every mistake possible. Most of those mistakes fall into two categories. First, I failed to establish boundaries—leading to numerous Spirit encounters for which I was unprepared. Second, I began to practice what I now call *psychic pouncing*. When I saw spirits around strangers, I blurted out what I heard, dumping out loads of data without asking for permission. I made these mistakes because I was showing off. To admit that I was a show-off stings. It is the hardest mistake for me to own.

It was harder to see that I was showing off in the beginning, and this is in part because these early fumbles led to situations that were more funny than harmful. I was utterly free of boundaries as I stood naked, drying my hair in our muggy bathroom. Then I heard a voice. "Hey! You're going to see my wife today. Hey! I need you to tell her something!" I nearly jumped. The voice was decidedly male, and it came from right next to me. Fresh sweat slid from my scalp and landed in the curves of my neck. Though I was becoming accustomed to Spirit contact, it still kind of freaked me out—and especially under the current circumstances.

After I heard him, I felt him. I knew I was home alone. But when I felt his touch, I dropped my blow-dryer faster than a lightning strike. Nobody was present. What touched my arm? As I'd never physically felt Spirit touch me before, I considered the possibility that the blow-dryer's cord was the culprit. Nothing seemed out of place, and the alternative felt creepy. I resumed drying my hair. Something tapped my upper right arm again—but this time, they were multiple slightly more forceful taps. *This is not my imagination! I felt that!*

"Hey! I'm so glad you can hear me! It's me! Jack. I need you to help my wife, Mary. She's having a really tough time grieving over me. She thinks I'm dead! But obviously, I am not. You could really help her. Remind her of our happy times together." Though I had never met Jack, I knew of him through Mary. He had transitioned, and Mary was inconsolable with grief.

Jack knew he had my attention. He became quite excited to get his message across. "I need you to remind Mary of the red muscle car I bought when we dated. I loved that car with the big HEMI engine. Remind her of how many times we took advantage of those bench seats! We made love so many times in that car—she'll remember that! We conceived our first child in that car! She hated that car after we had kids, but I always loved it. Please tell Mary to not cry so much. Please tell her I am around her all of the time—I wouldn't leave her! Tell her: *I am not dead!*"

Jack's palpable enthusiasm moved me. He too loved to remember intimate moments with his wife of forty years. Those specific details could really help ease his wife's intense grief. I telepathically told Jack that if the opportunity presented itself and the moment felt fitting, then I would share this information with Mary.

I was happy to deliver Jack's message to bring comfort to his grieving wife, and yet I found myself feeling really vulnerable. There I was, in my private bathroom, naked and drying my hair. Just a few months earlier, I'd started having contact with Spirit, and now it was happening all the time—and everywhere! *Can he see me? Does it work like that? This is insanity,* I thought. But it also felt almost normal; he was just Spirit, right? Despite my many rationalizations, I began to feel self-conscious. I telepathically communicated my concern. "Jack, I get it, but you shouldn't be here now! *I am naked!* This is really inappropriate. We need to talk about boundaries, Jack; this can't happen. You can't just pop up in my bathroom!" Jack's response still makes me smile because he suddenly broke into uproarious laughter. If he had a physical knee, he would have slapped it.

Though I had never known Jack in the body, this fit well with what I knew of him. Mary had always boasted about her husband's fabulous sense of humor. In his laughter, Jack quipped: "I know you're naked! Being in Spirit has so many benefits! This is so great! I can peep into a naked woman's bathroom without getting into trouble now!" As Jack continued to joke, his playfulness made me laugh out loud. And he still does that—because he has visited me many times since, and I now know him quite well.

I shared this first event with Mary later that same day. She confirmed every detail, laughing and crying at my recounting of his visit. When I shared Jack's flip response about appearing to me while I was naked, Mary smiled and said, "That sounds just like my husband! That's exactly what he would have said!" This event marked one of the definitive moments when Spirit appeared without my bidding—while I was butt naked.

Another time, the Spirit of Bruce appeared while I was taking a shower. I had met Bruce before—or, at least, I had met him in Spirit. Bruce's friend Ronnie was in my cancer support group. One day, he shared with the group that in addition to his diagnosis, he had been really struggling to accept the death of his lifelong best friend, Bruce. As the group ended that session, I announced that if anyone wanted to stay longer, I would offer a demonstration of mediumship. Everyone stayed. I meditated.

Suddenly, I saw a scene as if through someone else's eyes. It started with the expanse of beautiful blue-green ocean water. We were on a boat, and it was moving fast. I noted that Spirit was present. I saw wide, tan, bare feet, tanned skin, a big white smile, and light brown hair. It was Bruce. He provided other details, and Ronnie confirmed mostly everything—certainly more than the four pieces of evidence that I require from Spirit before delivering a message. At the time, I felt immense pleasure that I could be the messenger for Spirit. I felt comfortable communicating with him in that setting.

The next time he showed up, I wasn't quite as comfortable.

As I shaved my legs in the shower, Bruce appeared. Things got a little crowded! He began to rapidly show me scenes from his life. He showed me that while he was alive, parties didn't really get their groove until he arrived. He was *that* guy. Everybody loved Bruce because of his charm, good looks, and willingness to help a stranger. What most people did not know about Bruce is that he struggled with major depressive disorder. When things went well, Bruce ruled his world, but when the energy shifted—so did his mood. Bruce refused to get medication assistance to manage his symptoms. So he self-medicated with alcohol. During one of his depressive episodes, Bruce felt overwhelmed with life and all of its demands. He pulled out a gun and shot himself in front of someone.

There, in the shower, I understood the depth of Bruce's emotional inner turmoil. And he sent a message through me to deliver to Ronnie—a message about a nickname they used to find each other in a crowd. I heard Bruce say, "I used to shout to him from across the club, 'Zinny—over here!'" I texted Ronnie and told him about Bruce's pop-in visit. I could not wait to get confirmation if the nickname I heard in the shower was solid. It was.

I think it's natural to enjoy mediumship. Knowing psychic things about others and seeing their dead loved ones around them is crazy, mind-blowing fun! There is no other feeling in the world, for me, that elicits the same shockwaves of dizzy elation! Being a psychic-medium is a blast. It also feels incredibly good to bring so much peace to people. I *know* what it is to grieve. I have always wanted to be a channel that relieves suffering, and in those early days, I felt like a kid with a new superpower. I suddenly saw things; I knew the intimate details of events that others did not. I wanted to show everybody—family, friends, and especially those who doubted me.

Yet there is a downside to this enthusiasm. In my excitement, I found myself delivering information to complete strangers, some of whom may still be traumatized. Though the information was accurate, I often didn't wait to get people's full consent. I put my inflated ego before another's feelings. I regret this. It can be so harmful—not only spiritually but also emotionally. Later, I realized that this psychic pouncing was particularly dangerous because it potentially hurt others while benefitting me. I got to physically leave. I got my emotional needs met; I would just practice my mediumship skills, get affirmation, and walk away. I was like the hit-and-run medium. I dashed out, leaving the recipient to sort out and sift through very private and often painful information. In a professional psychotherapy capacity, I would never have done anything that would yield that sort of effect, but as a medium, I hadn't yet found the ethical line.

Once, following a psychic pounce, I heard secondhand that the recipient of my message cried for days afterward. This surprised me because the information I'd given her was fairly benign. It turned out that what spooked her was the invasion of privacy; like a peeping Tom, I was a voyeur into her life. I saw things that others did not know. My uncanny accuracy disturbed her—something I hadn't considered. In fact, she was creeped out precisely *because* the information was so accurate. I knew it was. I was excited by Spirit's specificity. I had a need to have it verified, and selfishly, I acted on that need. Hearing how it had hurt someone was a real wake-up call for me. In retrospect, I avoided setting boundaries because I wanted to see what spirits were hanging around. This experience showed me exactly what following that desire could cost. My previous psychic pouncing could really unsettle someone; my behavior had the exact opposite effect I had hoped. I hoped to use this ability to help people heal—instead, sometimes I hurt them.

When my bathroom started to get crowded, I recognized that I had to get a handle on my methodology. Now that I'd developed my gift, I had to develop the ethics around my delivery method, as well as some boundaries for contact. So I went back to review the training I'd received.

As I was taught, the medium defines the rules of engagement and hours of operation. Period. This agreement is a divine contract between the medium and spirits. This ensures that spirits cannot wake up the medium in the middle of the night, follow them around, appear uninvited, or endlessly chat. The medium is always in command. Whatever rules and boundaries the medium identifies, spirits must obey. This is the law of the universe.

As I stated before, a big part of me didn't want to establish these sorts of boundaries. I managed to talk myself out of doing so. At first, I'd thought that this instruction was about avoiding unwanted energies or those scary, Hollywood-style ghosts. This made it easy to dismiss, because in my experience, Spirit cannot harm anyone. They can be somewhat mischievous—they are, for instance, fully capable of making an object move or disappear—but that is only to get your attention; it's not intended to terrorize you. While other mediums suggest praying for protection prior to opening oneself up to the Spirit world, I merely ask my Spirit guides to allow only the highest energies access to me. My guides are my gatekeepers. In the hundreds of experiences with Spirit contact I have had, I have never seen anything even remotely scary.

Experience taught me that the emphasis on boundaries with Spirit doesn't come from the false fear that Spirit could be dangerous or scary. Instead, we need boundaries because our loved ones are so very desperate to make contact with us. Because Spirit is so eager to connect from across the veil, they use outrageous methods to get our attention. Their efforts to access a medium who can deliver a message to their loved one is impressive. This isn't because Spirit is doing anything wrong; a receptive medium is analogous to a neon Open sign. We need to tell Spirit what the rules are and when we are open or closed.

Anyone with mediumistic ability must also function in their immediate world. This time-space dimension demands that we interact with people who still inhabit their physical body. I know that sounds funny, but it's true; as embodied beings, we are primarily required to engage with spirits still tethered to their physical body—humans, because we are still on this side of the veil. As I worked to find the right balance between mediumship and everything else, I began to understand why James Van Praagh was stern with me after I giddily relayed my first Spirit contact: he was concerned about my mental stability. Though it was fun, it was also crazy-making to have Spirit chatting away and showing me images, and sending smells and physical sensations for me to process while I simultaneously tried to maintain a conversation with a living person. Being constantly open to Spirit contact was creating chaotic energy for everyone. I saw firsthand that when not properly tended, this beautiful gift can end up being more like a curse.

Beyond creating boundaries alone, I realized that the system I used to deliver information needed an update. I received training as an evidential medium, meaning I was taught to get a minimum of four specific pieces of evidence. This was relatively easy to follow: Data first, message second. The evidence must be nonfluffy, which is defined as concrete, specific, there-is-no-way-I-could-have-known-that data. Some unique details spirits have shown me include red shoes, sucking on lemons, red tulips, car accident details, exact physical location of gunshots, sucking on garlic, cherry pipe tobacco, favorite kind of red wine, country of origin, exact description of clothing, and even locations of sexual escapades! This type of data leaves little room for doubt for the recipient, regardless of how cynical they were before receiving it, and since I got this feedback immediately and directly, I was motivated to follow the instruction to provide it.

But I learned the hard way to adhere to other parts of what I was taught, such as to always ask the recipients permission prior to telling them what spirits were around them. Now, if I see Spirit around someone, I wait. If Spirit is around someone I already know, I say something like, "Hey, I think your father is here—do you want me to continue?" If I see Spirit around a stranger, I really wait. If I can strike up some kind of conversation, I attempt to assess their emotional stability. Then I may ask a casual question like, "Is your father still living?" Depending on how they respond, I might continue by asking if they know what a medium is and whether they are interested in some impressions I am receiving. So far, no one has ever told me no—but I still ask.

I also had to rethink my professional standards. As a psychotherapist, I have had many patients report visual or auditory hallucinations. Often, family members accompany the patient. A family member's input can be critical for clinical assessment and accurate diagnosis. Clinically, major depressive disorders and anxiety can create psychosis. That is, the patient reports that an invisible entity calls their name or appears "shadowy" to them. Talk therapy and medication intervention often resolve those symptoms. And, in this case—because they are, quite literally, *cases*—clinical symptoms brought on by severe depression or an anxiety disorder. However, I have had a few patients who appear, by my assessment, to truly be psychic-mediums.

When a patient reports symptoms that are consistent with both psychic and psychotic symptoms, it creates a professional conundrum. This is because it raises an ethical dilemma. Our first rule: do no harm. Beliefs, both those based in religion and otherwise, could cloud the lens the therapist uses to see the patient. As a clinician, I believe that some patients diagnosed with psychotic disorders may actually have psychic-mediumistic events occurring. What a cruel treatment-solution it is, then, to treat that patient with powerful antipsychotic medications.

On the other side, if a patient is truly psychotic, medication intervention saves lives—and sometimes more than just the patient's. Knowing that, it would be just as cruel to deny medications when appropriate. As a medium and a clinician, I've had to face this ethical challenge on several occasions. While the sphere of evidential mediumship is self-governed by the community, the sphere of professional psychotherapy adheres to a much more strictly enforced set of rules. So when these two worlds interact, I have to yield to the board-governed rules of my profession.

All of this helped me to develop a system based on the training I received, the professional standards I follow, and my personal set of ethics. In the end, despite my fears, developing my own system around my relationship with Spirit didn't reduce the amount of Spirit contact at all. Usually, Spirit finds me soon after I intentionally flash my neon green Open sign. Hundreds of spirits have appeared to me now, and they're all happy to follow my rules. In the four years since I was diagnosed with metastatic cancer, I've been able to deliver beautiful messages to people—messages that have brought them great peace.

Recently, I had to reinforce a boundary with a singing Spirit. I met my friend Michelle at her house. She volunteered to do some energy healing for me. While I was on the table, her deceased father appeared in Spirit. Michelle was a newer friend, and I was unaware of her family history. Her father provided specific evidence. But there is always a sort of coup-de-gras grand finale piece of evidence. It's like Spirit holds the best for last. This Spirit's final piece of evidence was a song. This Spirit began to sing, "Michelle, my belle ..." When I told Michelle, she burst into tears. It turned out her father sang this song to her all of the time!

This Spirit must have been thrilled that I could actually hear him and his beautiful voice. After I returned home, I began to make dinner. I had no idea this Spirit was with me until I heard him begin to sing. At first, I thought it was hilarious. But after an hour of his singing the same song over and over and over, what had previously been funny was now like fingernails on chalkboard. I gently but firmly told him he needed to go. He left immediately.

Having this opportunity to practice my boundaries affirmed once again that as the medium, I make the rules. I also get to decide how, when, and why I deliver messages. By doing this, I ensure that this powerful and beautiful thing—mediumship—doesn't hurt me or anyone who communicates with those beyond the veil. In return, I get to bring an incredibly healing gift into the world, and I get to use it purely in the service of love. This strengthens the connection with Spirit.

That's because love's indestructible spiritual plasma binds souls together—forever, always, and in all ways.

CHAPTER 5

Animal Spirits

> How it is that animals understand things I do not know, but it is certain that they do understand. Perhaps there is a language which is not made of words and everything in the world understands it. Perhaps there is a soul hidden in everything and it can always speak, without even making a sound, to another soul.
>
> —*Frances Hodgson Burnett*

My inner skeptic can be a bitch. Her critical, condescending comments contribute to my internal chaos. She said, *Nobody can talk to whales, Suzanne. Only crazy people think they can—and they're usually under long-term psychiatric care. Are you crazy, Suzanne? Which side of the psychiatrist's couch do you want to sit on—the patient's or the provider's? Be careful; it's a short distance between the two.* I sighed. Once again, I stood on the precipice between belief and disbelief. Do I jump? Or do I allow doubt to hold me hostage? The inner skeptic-bitch had more commentary to my internal thoughts. *You certainly could jump—and if you're wrong about the whale communication thing, one plausible explanation is that the cancer has gone to your brain. People would understand brain cancer, Suzanne. People could excuse your claim to talk to dead people and animals* ... But I'm entering in the middle of this story instead of the beginning.

Life was lively that morning. Everywhere I looked, life pulsed through the veins and arteries of Mother Earth. Earth spun on her axis and twirled around him, the sun. Their combined energy created the scaffolding for the day to build upon. Blue and green ocean water tangled with frothy foam. The white foam floated on top of the water and then, as if on cue, twisted to form baker-perfect meringue caps. Grandfather Ocean stretched out his arms and swam long strokes toward our boat until he caressed all sides of the vessel. The vessel welcomed his loving support.

Magic cast her favorable smile to everything above—and everything below—and the infinite space in between. The sun knew it was his turn to shine, so he nudged the shapeshifting clouds to evaporate. Without protest, the clouds conformed. The sun warmed the earth. Animals and insects created a harmonious cacophony that sounded like an orchestra tuning up their instruments before a performance. Their role was to provide background music that accompanies any good production. Seagulls pirouetted like aerial ballet dancers. Then they dove to pluck fish from the ocean's bounty. My attention turned to watch smaller birds chase insects. Insects played hide-and-seek with their predators and sought refuge with humans who waved them away. Even the wind contributed her gift to carry breezy scents of fish and flowers and salt water. Her role was to move things along and give the gift of scent. This supernatural oasis seemed to hold secrets of all creation.

It was a good day to live. It was a great day to be alive.

As our vessel departed Cape Cod's harbor, boat engines hummed their mechanical melody, transforming liquid fuel into vaporous fumes. The boat sped faster, which seemed to mirror a quickening of all of life. Sublime salt water sprayed my skin. I was startled, soothed, and then soaked with sensuous pleasure. Something sacred was percolating.

Cape Cod's waters brim with marine life. Tourists travel from faraway places to experience her majesty. Whale-watching excursions summon many vacationers, myself included, to willingly part with the paper or plastic content of their wallets in hope of accessing the divine in natural form. It was my first whale-watching trek. Our onboard scientist used a microphone to narrate various aquatic species to several hundred passengers who waited for something they too could see.

Before we departed that morning, the owner of the B&B where we stayed apologetically said, "Don't be too disappointed if you don't see any whales; it's been hit and miss this season." I hoped our trip would be on the "hit" side. We sailed until the coastline shrank to a dot. Two hours into our tour, the scientist announced the presence of whales. Passengers jumped and clumped together. We all violated social norms regarding personal space. Because this was an exception, everyone leaned on each other to catch a glimpse.

A hundred yards away, a few whales skimmed the salt water's surface. Anticipation escalated. We collectively held our breath as we waited to see that whale, any whale, but they all disappeared. It felt so quick that I wondered if I really saw them. I wanted more! Then, a barely visible whale swam just below the wavy water. It looked more like an inky-black oil spill that spread wide across the water. Then that whale began his opening act: he spewed a mountain-sized fountain of ocean water from his blowhole. He swam to build up more and more speed. It was difficult to see him, but that whale left a gigantic wake. So this is how the sailors' legendary sea-monster myths were born! My adrenalin quickened.

The onboard scientist excitedly told us that a juvenile whale was spotted. He instructed passengers to move from starboard to port side. The scientist added that this whale was a sixteen-year-old male. Apparently, whales have similar life spans to humans—so this whale was comparable to a teenaged boy. How can you make a wild whale swim closer to a passenger boat?

Ask. Ask the whale.

I did. Telepathically, I asked the whale to please come closer. I imagined shimmering emerald-green light shooting from my heart to his heart. Over and over again, I repeated this vision. I sent him love, and he responded. Yes, it is true. That whale answered me.

This juvenile whale telepathically responded to the energy of love. In my mind, I heard that whale say, "Stay here! Stay on this side of the boat. Don't go to that side of the boat—because I'm going to show off for you! Watch me!"

My husband tried to usher me to port side where everyone else waited. We were the only passengers standing on the starboard side. I resisted my husband's tug, whispering, "No, no, stay right here. He's going to put on a show for us. He just told me. Watch—really, he just told me that he's going to put on a show for us." Seconds seem like centuries when Spirit gives you a message that something is about to occur.

My husband looked at me. Although he believed in me and my psychic-mediumship abilities, communicating with whales was new to us both. We waited. Thirty seconds later, the young male whale jumped high and completely out of the water's deep waves. Over and over again, the young whale performed full breaches. The surprised scientist instructed everyone to return starboard to watch the whale's performance. I smiled at my husband and said, "See? I told you to stay on this side of the boat."

My patient husband lovingly responded, "Honey, I never doubted you." Now my husband and I stood fixed to the guardrail as passengers packed in like sardines behind us. That male whale continued in a performance that surpassed anything Sea World could create. His energy felt exactly like any human teenaged male with Olympic athletic ability.

He *wanted* to show off his skills. He *wanted* us humans to witness his strength. He *knew* exactly what he was doing. And he *loved* performing for us. During his final jump, he smiled at me. The whale telepathically said, "I'm so glad you heard me, I'm so glad you listened. I'm so glad you stayed on this side of the boat. Thank you for watching me. I hope you liked the show!"

Though it was the first time I'd communicated with a living whale, I'd long been communicating with animals in Spirit. A few years before, a middle-aged woman, Katherine, asked me to read for her. I knew nothing about her. How could I have known that her only "child" was a dead dog? When I sat in her presence, I could not see any human spirits around her. The only Spirit that appeared and sat right next to her was a dog. This black canine was a hefty boy who weighed at least a hundred pounds. He showed me how Katherine nearly always tied a red bandana around his neck. Then he telepathically told me that she took him everywhere in her vehicle. My inner skeptic-bitch laughed and said, *So … you're going to tell her that the only thing you see is a dog? This is going to be good.*

As unlikely as it seemed, this handsome dog continued to provide me with evidence. He showed me that he really wanted to sit on her lap when they rode in the car. He wanted to be as physically close to her as possible. But the steering wheel made this doggy's dreams difficult because he was too big to fit under it. He still tried to sneak as much of his bulky body around her as she drove. He loved his owner. He wanted me to tell her. Telepathically, I said, "Big canine boy, you are kidding, right?" I searched the energy fields for a sign of a human Spirit with whom to communicate. But the only Spirit I saw was a dog.

What if she's waiting to hear from a deceased child, or sibling, or spouse, or parent, and all I can see is a dog? This was another first for me. Spirit has taught me to stick with the messages they provide, regardless of how ridiculous it sounds to me. I'm only the messenger. I must accurately deliver what I'm told, even when it doesn't make sense to me. By that point, I was fully aware that any deviation from that ends in disaster.

Katherine appeared patient. As she sat in front of me, she quietly waited for me to give her something from a deceased loved one. *Anything.* In a nervous, hesitant voice that sounded too high pitched, I squeaked, "Um, well, I don't see any human spirits around you, uh, at this moment. However, a dog is here ..."

She leaned closer. I continued, "It's a male dog, and he's a good size. His fur is black ... he is showing me that he always had a red bandana around his neck."

Without notice, Katherine went from seemingly fine to frenzied. She doubled over in tears. *Oh boy, she's upset that I can't find her loved ones! What do I say now?*

Before my exit strategy formulated in my mind, she blurted, "Oh my God! I've never been married, I never had children, I only had a dog. I had this dog for seventeen years. I took him everywhere with me, including my vacations."

Phew! Really? Thank God; what I saw meant something to her. I gingerly asked another question—because I still was not convinced that the only being I could see was a dog. I asked, "Did you bring him with you in the car a lot?" She nodded. I said, "He's telling me that he always wanted to sit in your lap as you drove the car?" I phrased it more as a question than a statement because I was still uncertain about what I saw.

Katherine responded, "No, no!"

What? Oh boy, I'm all wrong.

She continued and said, "He was much too big for that. He couldn't have fit in my lap!"

Of course, this was precisely what the dog had told me too. With an affirmative nod, I said, "Yes, yes, I know—he was a big boy. But he's telling me that he still *wanted* to sit on your lap!" Her cries escalated to sobs as this evidence sent her into an emotional tizzy.

It may sound heartless, but as a medium, I sometimes take my cue from tears. When someone begins to cry or get emotional because of what I tell them, it's usually a sign that I'm giving them accurate evidence. That evidence translates to a big fat "Yes!" I feel both validated and relieved.

The last thing the dog showed me was that he loved his owner and was deeply grateful to her. He said, "Tell her I will be around her until she transitions. I will wait for her." I did, and her tears stopped. With wide-open eyes, Katherine looked at me. Her eyes mirrored my conflicted feelings of disbelief and belief.

All animals have spirits because all beings have spirits. Animal spirits appear to me in the exact same way as human spirits, and I know I'm not the only one to have this experience. What I don't know is *how* I connect with them, though I suspect it is the same way I connect to human spirits: through the vibrational network of love. I know that there are some people who have an uncanny ability to connect with animals but are not able to connect with human spirits, and vice versa. This mystery remains a conundrum to me. I do not pretend to know the answers; I only speak to my personal experiences.

Spirit is Spirit.

There is no such thing as death.

Nor is there much of a difference between the way we grieve our animals and the way we grieve other loved ones. Typically, animals appear for their loved one when a unique and tender bond was created while the animal was under human care. Their appearance is to help humans heal from their grief. Helping a loved one heal is always the goal of a Spirit appearance, regardless if they are in human or animal form.

Animals also send messages on levels that relate to our soul's healing. Pets and wild animals alike can serve as spiritual consorts. Birds—with their mercurial ability to move between heaven and earth—are one of our most spiritual consorts, and they have provided me with strong messages and guidance throughout my life. I'm not the only one who has experienced this, but I didn't fully understand it until they began to repeatedly deliver messages from my deceased loved ones. Now, every time I ask to receive a sign from a Spirit, all I need do is be in nature, and I am nearly guaranteed to find some type of gorgeous feather. Over the years, I have collected thousands of them. I consider them to be like love notes from the beyond.

During a period of intense grief after my brother's death, I began to experience clinical panic attacks. When a panic attack appeared, regardless of where I was, the only thing I could think about was where the nearest exit was located. This happened without much warning, frequently, and regardless of where I was. One time I was in a movie theatre, another time in my car, and another on an airplane. Before I experienced my own panic attacks, I did not fully appreciate what my patients experienced. Panic attacks are crazy making. I felt like a nut when they happened, and I probably would have been diagnosed as such if I followed my mind's suggestions. One time during a crowded flight, I started to feel claustrophobic. Panic overwhelmed me. My inner voice suggested that I crawl over all those passengers in front of me, open the exit door, and jump. Of course, I didn't do that—but I had to use every coping strategy I knew to breathe through the impulse to exit. One of my strategies, if I feel the onset of panic, is to go outside—get out in big, wide-open space and allow nature to enfold and comfort me.

One of those times, when I had to escape from the confines of walls and ceilings and tight spaces, I took refuge outside. I walked and walked and prayed for God to send me a sign that all was well. Miles into my walk, I looked down to step around something. That something was a huge, perfect hawk feather. God heard my prayers! I asked, and it was given. But my inner skeptic-bitch had to put her two cents in. She said, *If it's really a sign from God, He could do it again, right? Ask for something else.*

I challenged God and the Spirit world. I telepathically said, "Well, if you guys are really around me, I need something to hold my feathers." I continued to walk. Something caught my eye's attention. It was an abandoned bird's nest on the ground. I laughed out loud, thanking the Spirit world for not only putting up with my childish demands but also fulfilling them. Then I told my inner skeptic-bitch to take a hike.

Every time I request a feather, birds seem willing to provide them. A blue heron lives nearby. He knows me as I know him. Blue heron feathers are a rare find. But I wanted a feather to send to my Native American teacher, Johnny, a Hopi shaman who lived out west on the reservation. Johnny had an entire kiva of feathers. A blue heron feather for someone who lives in the desert would be a treasure. I walked by the heron, sending love from my heart to his, and I respectfully requested one of his feathers and explained it was for Johnny and would be an honored gift.

Several days later, I saw the heron. He telepathically told me, "I honored your request. I dropped and donated one of my feathers for the shaman. It's just over that hill, by the water." Seriously? I thanked that heron but waited until I actually found the feather. And, of course, my inner skeptic-bitch had to make her commentary. She mockingly said to me, *Hmm, so now you think you can talk to that heron?* I allowed her negative energy to instill doubt in me. I felt disheartened. I felt foolish to believe. I kept walking. Then I heard the heron: "Gawk, gawk, gawwwwkkk." I looked down.

Ten inches of gray-blue perfection sat there on the ground. That heron gifted me with a part of him—a fabulous feather. As that heron spread his six-foot wingspan and slowly rose to fly, I sent grateful love to him. Even as I type these words, part of this feels ridiculous—yet, it happened. It really did happen exactly the way I am sharing it with you.

Sometimes animals appear in Spirit when I am around their loved one. I attended a Christmas party with a group of my husband's peers. I was introduced to a woman named Jenny from Kentucky. We stood beside the appetizer and drink table. We went through the dance of casual conversation. As a psychotherapist, I am comfortable in these moments because I have had lots of practice making new patients feel at ease. The best ice-breaker is to ask open-ended questions. So, I started with the predictable stuff. I asked Jenny what took her to Kentucky.

Jenny, said, "I have a farm with horses."

Cheerfully, I responded, "Oh, you're living one of my not-yet-actualized dreams. I adore animals." I asked Jenny more questions about her farm. As Jenny provided details, she described something very upscale and posh. Not the simple farm I initially imagined. This Kentucky horse farm sounded elegant. In my mind, elegant equates to expensive. Somebody had money to run that caliber of a horse farm. In my head, I envisioned something from a movie set. I felt my own green-eyed monster appear—jealousy.

I wanted to step into her life for a little while. I wanted to own a regal horse farm. I wanted respite from my own cancer-riddled life. Instead, I stood before this well-coiffed woman and prayed that the bald spot on the crown of my head was still covered. I certainly showered it with stronghold hairspray. Brutal cancer treatment made some of my hair fall out and wounded my ego even more. But as I took a step away from my narcissism, I noticed that Jenny did not seem so happy. She, like all of us, had a story—some stories money cannot compensate for or comfort.

Her emotions shifted. Jenny stated, "My favorite mare just died. It may sound silly, but I loved that horse. She and I went through a lot together: the arrival of our adopted child, my mother's death, and my divorce! My husband left me for another woman. My life is in financial ruins. Everything is in shambles. The only thing that was consistently there for me was my mare. She was always there for me as a true companion."

Compassion replaced my previous jealousy. I suddenly saw, in my mind's eye, a gorgeous black mare galloping with Jenny in her saddle.

Then the mare spoke. Inside of my head, I heard the horse say, "I had a bad leg injury, and my leg never healed correctly. It was painful for me to carry my mistress on my back. But I did not care because I knew that she needed me. And I loved her. She was wonderful to me. I treasured our time together. We ran like the wind!"

Before I had time to weigh my next move, my inner skeptic-bitch spoke. With her demeaning tone, she demanded, *Do you have a glass of wine in your hand, Suzanne? Yes, you do. And now you're going to deliver a message from this woman's dead horse, a woman you just met, at a holiday party with your husband's peers? Go ahead, I dare you. People will think you're either drunk or nuts—probably both. Here goes your professional reputation. I can't wait to see how this ends …* Maybe this time my inner skeptic-bitch was right. Maybe I should just be silent.

Then I heard a different voice. This voice sounded infinitely kinder. The kind voice appeared to provide me with courage to counter my inner skeptic-bitch. The loving energy said to me, "Courage, courage, courage, Suzanne. Breathe. Trust. Deliver the message. Be willing to be wrong. It's worth it if there's a chance you could help ease this woman's emotional suffering." So I did it. I dared to look foolish if I could somehow help this woman's heart mend. I spoke.

Initially, I casually asked questions. I asked, "Your mare was black? And her coat was so shiny and beautiful! Is that right? Oh … I see that her back right leg was injured?" When this moment arrives, and the download of data I deliver is correct, people typically take a step backward. Jenny was no exception. When she finally spoke, she confirmed every detail. I silently thanked the kind, encouraging voice for pushing me toward trusting the message versus doubt.

Although I never owned a pet, I've dreamed of it. I even have pet names picked out. Owning a pet has been out of my reach for several reasons. First, when I served active duty in the US Air Force, owning a pet was a problem. Military personnel have a standard joke: "If the military did not issue it, you don't need it. That goes for spouses, children, and pets." The military does not accept the excuse of, "I can't go on that assignment because I don't have anyone to watch my dog, or my child." The military's response is typically something like: "Well, you'd better figure it out—because you *are* going." It may seem unfair, but today's military is voluntary, and everyone knows the rules before they sign the dotted line of their contract.

The second obstacle to pet ownership was that after my military service ended, my husband worked for a major airline company, and we wanted to use his employee benefits to travel before we started a family. Ironically, we chose destinations that were animal-packed. Scuba diving was one of our favorite hobbies; we dove in St. Thomas, the Florida Keys, and Belize. Owning an animal seemed impractical, yet we ended up in vacation destinations where we were surrounded by them.

Third, between graduate school and the multiple sudden deaths of loved ones, I found my energy completely sapped. Taking care of myself to get through the day was challenging. I felt I could not take on the responsibility of an animal. Throughout my childhood, we always had large Airedales, barn cats, and, at one point, horses. My mother spoiled our pets. She instilled in me that owning an animal is a serious commitment.

Although the timing never felt right for me to own an animal, somehow animals and I find each other. Neighborhood dogs and cats have sat at my back-porch door and waited for me to return home—sometimes so they could sit in my kitchen as I cooked or worked on the computer. But while I have always cared for animals, I have never loved animals as much as I do now. Since

I've been able to telepathically communicate with them, I am a sappy, sentimental lover of the entire animal kingdom.

And I know this: your beloved animals wait for you across the veil. The moment you exit your physical body to return home, your beloved animals greet you, just as your beloved humans do. This is because the guardian of your connection is love. *Love is the spiritual energy that eternally binds all beings*—and that has nothing to do with species. Love is like an enormous rainbow-colored web, and each of us is a strand. Every single shimmering strand is connected not only to each other and to all things but to God. God is at the center. When we understand this, it's easy to see how separation is an illusion—impossible.

CHAPTER 6

Discouraging Friends and Unexpected Support

> The intuitive mind is a sacred gift and the rational mind is a faithful servant. We have created a society that honors the servant and has forgotten the gift.
> —*Albert Einstein*

Billy-Bob is anything other than *a* Billy-Bob. Some people may think his name is too southern—which in the Deep South equates to a "he just a hick" or "boy be too country"—and not sophisticated. But Billy-Bob, although from the Deep South, was anything but unsophisticated.

Our first meeting was at the shampoo bowl at an upscale hair salon. He introduced himself and with a strong southern drawl said, "Hey, I'm Billy-Bob, but you can just call me Billy."

But there's much more to Billy-Bob—Billy—than his name.

Billy's body is the perfect playground. His physique made "inkers" want to hone their skills. Tattoos don't enhance Billy; Billy enhances tattoos. Some people just seem to wear that look very well. Billy wears it well. But this story is about something so much more beautiful than Billy. This first story underscores how Spirit can speak from anywhere—from any form. This time, *Spirit spoke from the womb.*

I confess. I assumed that because Billy worked at a popular hair salon and wore fabulous fashion-forward clothes, he was probably gay. This was the first time I met him. As I lay back in the leather chair, he guided my head to fit the neck holder in the shampoo bowl. He gently removed foils from my hair. Each one dropped into the porcelain sink with a hollow "clink." Billy massaged my scalp, washing my hair with perfect pressure. I relaxed. Then *it* happened. Familiar exquisite colors of cobalt blues and emerald green began to swirl behind my closed eyes. Spirit was present. Then I saw something that I have never seen before, or since:

I saw an unborn baby.

I saw an unborn fetus in utero. It was happily suspended in the mother's amniotic fluid. I saw the baby's translucent skin, large eyes, and the umbilical cord. The baby swayed in the mother's womb. It's a good thing I was already in a horizontal position, because this scene was both so weird—yet so fascinating—I could have fainted. This event shocked me so much that if the colorist had not been adding color to my hair, it may have instantly turned white. I have communicated with spirits of dogs, horses, whales, cats, birds, and even a snake. I have communicated with spirits of people who have "died." But an unborn fetus, still in utero, induced an emotional shockwave big enough to create a tsunami.

My anxiety climbed vertical like a nuclear missile. I did not rationally think, *Oh, how lovely—I see an unborn baby still in the womb!* Instead, my internal skeptic-bitch screamed, *I don't care if our hair falls out! We need to get out of here! Now! These chemicals must be making us crazy! Run! Get out!* Only now, after nearly four years of communicating with spirits, do I feel modestly comfortable. This still-in-utero fetus looked more like a science project than human, and it felt too bizarre, even for even me.

When I thought things could not get crazier, they did. The fetus calmly said, "That is my daddy."

I felt awkward, yet I telepathically answered, "Uh, okay, honey ..."

The fetus sweetly added, "I'm a girl." From her casual tone, she sounded like this happened all of the time—an unborn fetus talking to a strange woman while her father-to-be washed someone's hair. Sure. That's normal. This fetus sounded as if our conversation held no mystery at all. The baby-in-utero science project said to me, "Will you tell my daddy that I am here and waiting to be born? I love him ... very, very much." She did not say that she *would* love him but that she already *did,* as if she had known and loved him for a thousand years. It felt like they were old friends rekindling their bond.

The baby telepathically said, "And I really like the pink flowers he and my mommy planted last weekend. Tell him thank you." In my mind, she showed me beautiful pink flowers. She showed me how her mommy worried about her weight, jiggling her upper arms as she complained to her husband that she was too fat. She showed me that her mommy had very blonde hair as she added, "It isn't real ... but she likes it that way." Finally, she showed me the moment of her birth—something she was still waiting to experience yet seemed to have already seen. Her father picked her up and held her high. I could feel his intense joy as she felt the familiar, loving hands of her father.

I felt very unsure about this Spirit interaction. For one thing, I was communicating with a fetus—something I had not even imagined possible, although, at this point, I was a semi-developed psychic-medium. For another, what this sweet baby Spirit showed me was her mother and father doing something as simple as gardening. But beyond that, I was concerned because what she showed me conflicted with my first impression—that Billy was gay.

Billy's warm voice and cold water jolted me at the same time. "Going to do a cold-water rinse now." The energy shifted as I was tugged back into my earthly reality. With feigned indifference, I asked Billy if he had any children. Billy's slow southern drawl was as smooth as Tennessee whiskey. He said, "Yep, I sure do."

Delicately, I said, "This may sound weird … do you have a partner who is pregnant?"

Billy said, "Yep. My wife is pregnant with our fifth child."

Their *fifth* child? I retracted my original assessment—not only was I off, I was *way* off! *Clearly*, I mused, *Billy has been a very busy non-gay guy.*

I told Billy about my mediumship and asked him if I could share what just happened. Billy nodded as I recounted nearly everything. Billy did not seem surprised; it appeared he had already heard about me from others in the salon. I asked him if he and his wife recently planted pink flowers in their garden. His look said it all. "Yep. We were in the garden this past weekend and planted pink flowers." He casually wrapped my wet hair in the towel. As he ushered me from the shampoo sink to the stylist's chair, I turned around. I looked at him and boldly stated, "You know, it's a girl."

Billy stared at me hard. It felt as if we were playing a poker game. Seconds passed as he considered his next move. Then he allowed his emotional guard to drop. Billy said, "Wow. My wife and I literally just found out—I mean a few hours ago! They told us that it's a girl." That sealed the deal, validating everything I previously shared.

I could not wait to share this story with my friends. Not only could I communicate with the dead people and animals, I had verifiable proof of communication with a fetus! I expected my family and friends, some of whom identify themselves as religious conservatives, would welcome these divine, miraculous experiences.

But when I shared them, only silence hung in the space between us. I was naïve. After all, these same remarkable friends walked with me through hell and back; they stood by me through every scan, every round of chemo, every round of radiation, and everything else done to my body in the name of cancer treatment. My friends were, and continue to be, like a stellar military unit assigned with a difficult mission. They had my back. They had my back—until I started to see dead people. Spirit contact stories crossed boundaries with many people's religious beliefs. A few of them made it clear that they felt unable to support me, while others just slowly backed away. And, in retrospect, I do not blame them. How does anyone respond when someone begins to make claims that they see and talk to dead people?

To me, mediumship felt like sweet compensation for all of my prior emotional suffering and current physical pain. Though I had agonized over my loved ones' sudden deaths and now faced potentially fatal cancer, God came to repeatedly show me that *death is an illusion*. God did not whisper this to me—He gave me example after example of evidential Spirit contact.

After overhearing me share some of my experiences of Spirit contact, one woman boldly approached me and warned, "You know, what you're doing goes against what scripture says. The Bible says you should not be conjuring up the dead!"

Everyone stopped talking; this was good gossip unfolding. I paused and then said, "Yes, I understand that some people feel this way. But what if these messages help people to heal—people who have suffered a terrible loss—isn't that a good thing? The information I deliver is accurate and undeniable evidence that death is an illusion; it's not an attempt to bring the dead back to life."

In self-righteous rigidity, she cautioned, "Yes, well you know … Satan is very tricky."

Oh, God. I did not have energy to dispute ridiculous claims. I gulped hard and mumbled, "Yes, I'm sure Satan can be tricky indeed."

Though no one in my close community was nearly as aggressive about their beliefs, discouraging words from several people fell heavy on my heart like a rock. There are so many questions I still cannot answer within myself—how can I answer them to other people? For instance, I do not understand how or why I am permitted to see spirits. My ability does not make me an expert on religion or spirituality; I am only an expert on my experiences, and even I doubt some of them. Sometimes I cannot believe a Spirit contact event really happened. When I process my gift with supportive friends and my therapist, I allow myself to question it: *Maybe I'm just making the whole thing up ... or maybe I'm just a really good guesser! I'm a therapist, I sit with people all day—maybe I just read people well, and some things are highly predictable. Plus, you don't have to be a psychic or medium to be correct ...* Internal skepticism and doubt are always at the ready, and they feed my fear that the community in which I live and work professionally will identify me as crazy or evil.

But then how do I explain how I get these exact, specific, concrete, verifiable details about complete strangers? My left-brained husband—a military academy graduate with a BS in engineering, an MS in computer systems, a professional airline pilot with a Mensa card too—continues to provide a strong source of support to help keep my doubt at bay. He is frequently with me when Spirit appears. After the Spirit contact is over, I often share my doubts with him, but he reassures me every time because he *sees* it happen. He sees the evidence land; he sees the reaction.

He has also seen how these events weave into my own experience; he's seen how sometimes my own life lines open me to Spirit's message in the hours and days preceding a contact. Perhaps Spirit has a hand in this, preparing me to understand the message I'll be asked to deliver.

On one such occasion, we traveled to North Waters, Canada, to retrieve our son. This remote island is accessible only by boat or floatplane. It feels like a world away from our home in Atlanta. Our teenaged son participated in a canoe trip, the St. James Bay expedition. St. James Bay abuts next to the Arctic Ocean, which invites some challenging conditions, and thus the canoe trip serves as a rite of passage designed to test honor and build confidence in young people.

My husband and I were determined to be there when our son returned. As we stood on the boat dock with other parents, we watched our youth paddle their canoes into the harbor's entrance. It was like a movie scene. Dozens of tribal drums beat their slow, steady rhythm from the shore. This ceremonial ritual is like a welcome beacon for the canoe team. A hush holds the silence. I spotted our beautiful boy; he was too thin, tan, very dirty, and covered in mosquito bites. What a profound moment. The magic moment evaporated when I felt a sharp pain in my back molar. Ouch! What was that?

We traveled for several more days. I purchased ibuprofen and oil of clove to mitigate my molar pain. I considered seeing a local dentist, but I noticed many people were missing teeth! I wanted my tooth repaired, not extracted. Throughout our travels, my husband dutifully heard my complaints of pain. Of course, neither of us realized that it was the lead-up to a Spirit contact. When we got back to Atlanta, my dentist referred me to an endodontist, Dr. Smith. She came into the procedure room and introduced herself. The only things on the colorless walls were diplomas from Harvard Medical School. The sterile space was void of any personal photographs.

As I lay horizontal in her dental chair, I felt helpless. I prayed that she knew what she was doing to fix my aching molar and was hoping to receive some warmth and reassurance in the process. But Dr. Smith presented as introverted and all business. By now, the molar was infected, and that infection spread into my sinus cavities. When she reclined the chair, infected fluid drained down my throat, which made me choke, and instinctively, I jerked my head up. If she felt compassion, I did not sense it.

Dr. Smith and her assistant quietly worked. I prayed. I asked God to give her wisdom to fix my molar. I followed prayer with meditation and opened up all of my chakras—ancient known energy points in the body. When I got to my heart chakra, I imagined emerald-green light flowing from my heart to both Dr. Smith and her assistant. I sent them both love. In truth, I didn't do this because I am so spiritually advanced; I did it because I wanted optimum treatment. Emerald-green light shifted from a linear line to the shape of a number eight on its side—the symbol for infinity. Hard tooth shards flew around my mouth and onto my face. The foul odor of infection motivated me to continue meditating. Repeatedly, I sent them the emerald-green infinity symbol.

Spirit appeared.

This was the Spirit of an older woman. Spirit said, "That is my niece," indicating to Dr. Smith. She flashed images to show me how she looked.

Because I needed confirmation, I said, "So you are her aunt? Am I clear that you're not her grandmother?" She confirmed she was an aunt.

Spirit calmly continued to provide evidence and stated, "I died from cancer."

I acknowledged that I heard her and said, "Oh, I'm sorry. I've had cancer too. How old were you when you transitioned?" She answered that she was sixty-eight and that her name started with an M. I asked her to repeat it, because I knew that Dr. Smith's first name also began with an M, and I wanted to make sure I was not confusing their names. With infinite kindness and patience, she repeated the evidence to me again. I really liked this woman. Her energy was the exact opposite of her niece's stern and serious demeanor.

Spirit balked at this, and I realized Dr. Smith's aunt had heard my thought! I tried to recover and said, "I'm sorry, I don't mean to be disrespectful, but your niece doesn't seem anything like you!"

Spirit smiled and replied, "I tried to show her that she must not limit her understanding to only Western ideas—there are so many other ways to help people heal! When I lived in the physical, I exposed her to other ways of believing, but she is so resistant. I remain around her now to help her—to put new ideas and thoughts into her consciousness. I loved her when I was in the physical, and I love her now. We were very close."

Time felt suspended as we continued to communicate. Spirit flashed visual images to show me how she appeared on the physical plane. I saw that she was above average height and very slender. She wore fitted shirt-waist dresses. But the coolest piece of evidence she both showed me and said was, "See, do you see my hair? Although I relaxed it, I never colored it. I did not need to because it remained dark—except this one area. Everyone knew me by this thick white 'skunk' streak in my bangs." Wow! I did see it! What a unique piece of evidence!

Then Spirit shifted from her appearance to tell me details of her life. She added, "I never married. I fell in love, but someone broke my heart, and I never fell in love again. My mother and I lived in a big home together. I was a spiritual seeker." To illustrate this point, she showed me the image of a Bible. Erroneously, I assumed that meant she identified herself as a Christian. That would be my mistake later when I disclosed evidence to Dr. Smith.

Spirit continued with something very important she wanted her niece to know. "You must tell her that I am around her and I love her. But what she really needs to know is that I am also around her son. I watch over them both. He needs guidance right now. He needs my help because he is doing things he should not be doing." She went on to explain behaviors that would concern any mother. I was raw from my experience with my own son from the past weekend, and this touched me deeply. Spirit continued with critical information. "Tell her that when she leaves for work in the morning, her son goes out to buy drugs. Sometimes I interfere: I hide his wallet. I move it so he does not have any money. I also prevent his car from starting so he does not have transportation to his dealer. Please tell her I am here. Tell her everything I have shown to you. She needs to know these things."

I found it beautiful that Spirit worked with diligence to help this boy from harm and to warn his mother—her niece. I wanted to continue my conversation, but then someone else spoke. It was Dr. Smith. The procedure was over, and I felt like I had to deliver this message—but how could I get Dr. Smith to accept it? I doubted she would ever believe me.

I hesitated before casually asking, "Do either of you have an aunt who died of cancer?" Dr. Smith nodded in affirmation, staring at me. My neurotic babble took charge. I said, "I know this is going to sound really weird, but I see dead people ... well, um, you know, spirits. I mean, I haven't always seen them. I'm not crazy or hallucinating ... I don't do recreational substances or anything like that either—really, I don't! I work for a psychiatrist, I mean, for like a long time, so if I were psychotic, he would know. Anyway, I know this is really weird, but um ... your aunt was here. She was right here."

Dr. Smith did not speak. Her assistant appeared immobile. My face flushed. Then I forced my mouth to stop moving. Because the more I spoke, the crazier I sounded. I already knew that Dr. Smith did not believe in such things—her aunt had told me. I realized I better begin to give the evidence or I would be dismissed as a nut. Then they would politely usher me to the payment window where I would be tagged in their computer system as a DNR, which is code for Do Not Reschedule. So I started filling in the details. I said, "Your aunt told me her name beings with an M sound. I don't know if that's her last name, but it feels like her first name." The silent doctor sternly nodded. I continued and said, "She died of cancer when she was around sixty-eight. She was tall and thin, and she enjoyed fashion."

The skeptical doctor nodded, and with a bare whisper, she said, "This is amazing …"

Then, like so many other recipients of these messages, the doctor stepped back. Except in this case, she was on a roller chair, so she just rolled it away from me.

I explained everything that Spirit showed me. Dr. Smith responded with quiet shock. Her persona softened as she whispered, "This is amazing … amazing! I can't believe this." She confirmed her aunt's name. "Her name was Miranda. I can't believe this—there's no way you could know that!" For someone who couldn't believe it, she seemed to be getting pretty close.

She told me that her aunt lived in New Orleans and was very spiritual throughout her life, and I replied, "Oh—that's why she kept showing me a Bible."

Suddenly, there was a lurch in the energy in the room. My misinterpretation nearly invalidated everything. Dr. Smith rolled her roller chair even further away from me, and this time, it felt far more like mistrust than shock. Defiantly, she said, "No, you are wrong. She was not a Christian." The flat persona returned. Everything I shared suddenly sounded ridiculous. Dr. Smith gave me a look as if to say, *You nearly fooled me.*

From what I've seen, Spirit can only use imagery that already exists in my mental library of knowledge and experience. For instance, Spirit will reveal an accent while transmitting in English instead of a foreign language I cannot understand. When the Spirit of Aunt Miranda showed me a Bible, I assumed she meant she was a Christian. Spirit flashes images of things that I will easily and quickly understand to get me turned in the right direction. But sometimes the image is not literal. In this case, she was representing the image of spirituality that was most familiar to me.

I explained all of this to Dr. Smith. Once she understood that the image was metaphorical, and the energy in the room calmed once more, she said, "Yes, she was very spiritual; she had religious statues all over her house." Phew. Crisis averted. We were back on track. I further explained that if Aunt Miranda had showed me statues, I may have misinterpreted that to mean she had been a sculptor, or an art collector, or an art dealer. This explanation made sense to Dr. Smith.

I added an important message from this beautiful Spirit of Aunt Miranda. "And part of what your aunt wants you to remember is that while the allopathic model of medicine is good, it is limited. There is so much more. She showed you, and she said that you know this; the universe is enormous and so magnificent. Healing can take many paths. Do not be overly invested in what you learned at school." Dr. Smith nodded. She understood.

Finally, I shared the difficult part of the message that Aunt Miranda wanted her niece to know. It was also the part of the message that the mother in me most wanted to pass along. I asked, "You have a son, right? You have a teenaged son? He's making some poor choices; you know what I mean, right?" The doctor confirmed she had a son and was worried about him. I said, "Your aunt wants you to know that she's around him, she's watching out for him. And when he goes to do some things that he should not be doing, she interferes." Dr. Smith began to cry. We both understood maternal pain and worry, and we could relate to each other on that plane. I wondered if this was the reason for my dental problems in the first place: there I was, feeling the depth of motherhood, when my tooth began to hurt. In healing it, I got to share that depth with another. Perhaps Aunt Miranda summoned me as I stood there on the dock, clapping for my son.

I have been blessed to watch several people overcome serious doubt like Dr. Smith did. Yet still others hold to their own spiritual truths, which is fully within their rights—as long as they're not messing with what I know to be true. Luckily, unexpected support also arrived, and it provided me with titanium-like strength to speak my truth. I continued forward, bolstered by the support of my husband and my spiritual mentors. Then, additional help arrived in human form called Brian Weiss, MD.

Through a curious set of synchronistic events, I ended up seated next to Brian for dinner. I am a huge fan of his books, and I was very excited. Spirit contact stories gushed from my mouth like a broken dam. I saw and heard myself talk nonstop about my astounding experiences. I was so animated I could not eat. I realized I was not hungry for tangible food; I was starved for spiritual validation. When my verbal flood softened to a trickle, Brian calmly suggested that perhaps holding this energy back had greater potential to kill me than cancer. He encouraged me to speak my truth, citing all the people that could be healed by the messages I transmit. Brian was right, and his words marked a turning point for me. He shone light and clarity to my internal, murky darkness. I knew I could not allow fear and doubt to stop me from sharing my experiences.

If I can help ease someone's suffering, I have to continue. I must share these experiences in an effort to help grieving hearts heal. These events are true. Life after death is real. Spirit contact events are not a fantasy fairy tale—they are fact. Your loved ones want you to really know these truths. I cannot die silent.

Today, I continue to walk forward in my truth, telling the world what I know: that death is an illusion and that only love is real. Many people doubt this gift—including me, at times, as I continue to have new experiences that test the boundaries of possibility, as I did with Billy and his daughter-in-utero. Some of them are determined to believe what they believe, despite any evidence to the contrary—and on occasion, they're quite vocal with their discouragement! Others, like Dr. Smith, are changed when a Spirit contact touches their heart. Still others, like Brian Weiss (and hopefully, one day, me!), can help encourage mediums who are developing their skills by pushing them out into the world. This unexpected support provides strength to the parts of us that still struggle with doubt. It pushes us to speak anyway, because it's our calling.

So I do. I speak for all spirits who have appeared to me—not *for* me *but for you.*

CHAPTER 7

Spirit Is Relentless

> The most beautiful things in the world cannot be seen or even touched, they must be felt with the heart.
> —*Helen Keller*

Curvaceous bulbs begged to be planted in the Georgia red clay. A bag of bulbs burst at the hem, as if they too were happy with anticipation. It was my first time to plant tulips. Getting dirty and gritty in the southern soil helped manage my anxiety. My anxiety escalated because I was in the middle of another chemotherapy trial, and the day of the MRI that would reveal whether I would live or die crept ever closer.

When I work with the earth and plants and flowers, it's as if some spiritual vortex spins around me, and I feel blissfully giddy. God's artwork manifests through blooms of foliage and flowers. Many tulip bulbs found their new home in the soil that afternoon. I felt satisfied with the progress I made, measured by the mounds of freshly planted bulbs and the gritty orange clay under my jagged fingernails. The remaining bulbs and dirt were temporarily deserted due to a scheduled Reiki session. I was entirely unaware that those tulips were a celestial sign that would usher in the appearance of Spirit.

My colleague and friend, Liza, offered to do Reiki on me. I welcomed any alternative practice to stave off the multiple malignancies that took residence on many major organs. Liza asked her student, Katrina, to assist. I knew Katrina casually. Details of her personal life were unknown to me, but we had interacted a bit in the past. Katrina's tall, sultry body framed her Irish features. Despite her attractive smile and charming brogue, I sensed she was not a pushover. I slid under the warm blanket, and our session began. Liza and Katrina silently worked. I meditated and quickly relaxed.

Spirit appeared. In my mind's eye, a woman Spirit presented herself. She identified herself as Katrina's mother. The first thing she showed me was her flawless skin. She swept her hand over her face and confidently stated, "I never had acne like the other girls. Isn't my skin beautiful?"

I responded, "Uh, Yes, yes—very lovely." I had never had a Spirit emphasize their skin, or specifically their beauty before. Spirit continued to telepathically communicate information about her life and flashed images to me in a slide-show fashion. While she lived in her physical body, she was known as good-looking, and she wanted me to understand. This would prove to be significant to her daughter Katrina, and Spirit is relentless when communicating evidence. Then Spirit showed me her teeth.

She did so to communicate that she did not like her smile. She warned me of how this evidence would be received, stating, "When you tell my daughter this, she will deny that I had any flaw in my teeth. She will say that I had a beautiful smile. Although most people thought my smile was perfect, I didn't like this ..." She pointed to her front tooth where there was a tiny brown spot. She had always been self-conscious about that spot. She added, "I wanted it corrected, but I was concerned it would ruin my jawline." Though this last statement didn't make much sense to me initially, she presented herself in post-WWII attire, so perhaps at that time the tooth would have just been extracted. She showed me many other specific and personal details. Some of the other details were about Katrina's current health challenges, which Spirit told me that she could easily cure with simple dietary modifications. But at the end of the abundant evidence she provided, this Spirit gave a final parting gift for her daughter: she showed me an enormous armful of magnificent red flowers. This was an important detail.

Sometimes when Spirit shows me images, it is as if I am looking through a foggy window. It is not always clear. It takes intention on my part to visually focus. Loving Spirit will patiently flash an image multiple times until I understand. If I have trouble seeing something, then Spirit will show the same scene over and over again. It is like adjusting the focus on binoculars. I could not bring the large bouquet into full focus. I telepathically said, "I see they are red flowers. Are those roses?"

Spirit indignantly responded, "Oh heavens no! I didn't care for roses at all! Actually, I hated roses!" I thought, *Who hates roses?* Then the image came into perfect focus. Tulips. Spirit held an armful of red tulips. These tulips were a gesture of love for her daughter and very significant.

When the Reiki session finished, I felt ambivalent about telling Katrina. *Do I tell Katrina? Or do I keep quiet?* When this occurs, I carefully weigh whether the information will be healing or hindering. The answer is seldom clear-cut. To share what I see in Spirit, I have to take both a leap of faith and a calculated risk. Luckily, my clinical training as a psychotherapist serves this end. For example, if I had any hint that somebody could be mentally unstable or have a psychotic disorder, I would zip it. I thought about what I knew of Katrina from our few interactions in the past. I rolled the dice. I took a chance. I told Katrina.

I told Katrina I believed I had communicated with her mother during the session, and I began to share the details her mother had provided to me. Like always, I started with the evidence first; otherwise the message will not be believed. I told Katrina about her mother's beautiful skin, her fabulous figure, and something about her smile she didn't like. Katrina cautiously listened to my experience but naturally held doubt. I would too. But when I told Katina about her mother's discolored tooth, I had her attention. And, of course, Katrina responded *exactly* the way her mother predicted.

Katrina defensively stated, "My mother had a beautiful smile, but she had one small brown spot from a childhood illness. Nobody could see it but her. She always wanted it corrected but was concerned the correction could ruin her jawline." Now that I had her buy-in, I felt compelled to share the other message her mother had shared with me. Even though Katrina presents as physically fit and healthy, some part of me doubted what Spirit showed me. I referenced the digestive issues Katrina's mother had told me about, and I passed on her recommendation to cut back on the diet sodas. Katrina became more visibly shaken and teary as she recognized the specific pieces of evidence.

But I had no idea the final piece of evidence would prove to be the most profound: the red flowers.

I said, somewhat casually, "The last thing your mother showed me was a big armful of red tulips. I don't know why she was so specific that they were tulips, but she was! At first, I thought that maybe they were red roses but—"

Katrina interrupted and excitedly stated, "No, no, no, they could not be roses! My mother would never give me roses. My mother hated roses! One time, my father grew roses, and she made him rip them out."

I thought that was pretty weird—making someone rip roses out of the ground. I said, "Yeah, she indicated that she didn't care for roses at all."

Katrina said, "Suzanne, this is absolutely incredible! You would not have any way of knowing this: *my father had a tulip farm in Holland.*"

I thought, *Wow! A tulip farm? In Holland?* Now I was speechless.

Before the day's sun disappeared so that nighttime could make her entrance, the last of the tulip bulbs beckoned me to return. The cool clay felt good beneath my fingers. Returning to Mother Earth helped emotionally ground me after the spontaneous contact with Spirit. I marveled at Katrina's disclosure regarding her father's tulip farm. I knew nothing of her father and certainly had no idea that he had owned a tulip farm in Holland. Actually, I don't think I have ever met anyone who owned a tulip farm in Holland. It seemed so wild that I'd been planting the tulips before I even saw Katrina—as if somehow her parents were whispering to me from beyond.

I picked up a naked bulb and examined it. It was as if I were truly seeing it for the first time. Those voluptuous bulbs I plucked from the bag and planted in the earth hours earlier were just tulips. In such a brief time, those tulips transitioned into treasures. The tulips now represented the treasures I gained because Katrina and her mother bestowed an enormous blessing on me. Like so many mothers and daughters, they were desperate to contact each other. I was the conduit for their connection.

My knees slightly sank into the wet soil as I reached around to collect small bits of trash to tidy the garden. I marveled at the power of love. Love seems to be like spiritual superglue that eternally binds us. Love tethers us together forever. Time, Spirit reminds me, does not exist. Time is a man-made concept. I do not pretend to understand or grasp this concept—I only know what I have been shown.

Mothers and daughters have an unbreakable bond. I had the same with my own mother, and in part, my admiration and love for her led me onto this path. I have had the opportunity to make this connection between several mothers and daughters. One of them, which occurred when I was quite new to delivering these messages, arrived third-hand and decades after the daughter's transition. Spirit's clever persistence seems to have no limits. Like

Katrina's mother, this Spirit was desperately trying to contact the ones she'd left behind.

A little girl was killed during a holiday parade. But before I knew those details, she appeared to me in Spirit while I was in a hotel shower. I felt her presence, but it wasn't strong enough to allow direct communication. And since this event took place early on in my experiences, I felt more skeptical and doubtful of what I saw and heard. I got out of the shower and prepared myself to spend the day at a workshop on developing mediumship. I felt a migraine headache developing, which made it difficult to focus. Maybe the hotel gift shop would be open and sell analgesics. I needed to tame the oncoming migraine before it immobilized me from throbbing pain and vomiting. The small store offered a limited selection. I prayed the migraine would vanish.

I arrived at the workshop just as our instructor gave us our next assignment. The class broke into small groups of ten people each. The goal was to stand in front of your group, tune into whatever psychic or Spirit impressions you received, and see if anyone in the group could identify the information. Each person took their turn, and everyone did remarkably well. I was amazed! It was my turn. My headache and I stood up. Nine participants patiently waited. They were supportive and kind as they waited for me. Nothing happened. Then something did happen. The little girl who appeared earlier in my shower was back.

That little girl appeared in Spirit. She telepathically told me she was seven years old. She flashed visuals, and I saw her long brown hair with thick bangs. I felt her childlike energy. She showed me she owned a pony. Her pony looked like a pinto with tan spots against a white coat. She flashed more images as she sat on the pony in front of a white house with black shutters and a big front porch. There was a red barn behind her. She was so proud that she was old enough to ride a real pony. She showed me she wore blue jeans topped with new suede chaps.

Her fingers played with the fringe. She said, "Grandma bought these chaps for me, for my special day."

I telepathically said, "Wow, honey, you look adorable!"

Then she showed me her shirt. She said, "I get to wear a shirt with buttons, like a big-girl shirt. Can you see my buttons? I am so happy Mommy bought me a real big-girl shirt with buttons!" I told her that I could see everything she shared. The button-down shirt seemed very important to this little-girl Spirit, as she mentioned it over and over again.

I presented everything the child showed me. I looked around at my group. My group looked around at everyone else and then back at me. Although my classmates really wanted to help me out, nobody knew this child. Nobody could place her. Ugh! How embarrassing. Everyone else had something that somebody claimed. Not me. I was a hero at zero. My throbbing head and I sat down. I felt deflated and humiliated. My inner skeptic-bitch couldn't pass up this opportunity. She said, *Why are you here? This is stupid. What a waste of time and especially money. You clearly do not have any psychic or mediumship ability.* Inner skeptic-bitch got me—I wanted to cry. Class ended for the day, and we were scheduled to resume the next morning. Fine with me. My head felt like it held a jackhammer inside.

The next morning, my migraine had softened somewhat. Our instructor asked us to repeat yesterday's assignment but with a different mix of people. It was my turn. I stood up, and my migraine pain shot up. I apologized to my peers that I didn't feel on my game. I said to my group, "Sorry, I know some of you were in my group yesterday, and I talked about the seven-year-old girl with the pony. Well, she is back again."

A kind classmate gently said, "Suzanne, just stay with it; this Spirit is here for a reason, and there must be some connection or she wouldn't keep appearing to you. Go ahead and ask her to share her story."

The little-girl Spirit repeated the previous day's evidence, which I repeated to the group. The child told me that she transitioned twenty years ago. Then Spirit showed me something she had not shown me the day prior. The girl showed me she was in a hospital bed and her arm had multiple IV tubes coming out of it. She showed me that she had a terrible headache.

Suddenly, it began to sink in: I was experiencing *her* headache. Her pain was one of the ways she could let me know that she was around. I did not understand this then, but I do now. Spirit will show me how they physically felt to get their point across. I have felt heart attacks, strokes, being shot, and car accidents. It was not that Spirit tried to hurt me; they were overly zealous to demonstrate to me how they died so that I could present that evidence to their loved one. The quickest way to communicate a message is through physical feeling—how could words or pictures compete with that?

Then I heard this darling little girl try to tell me her name. She said, "And my name is, MMMMMmmmmmmaaaar, my name is MMMMMmmmeeeezzzz." Then she showed me how frightened and confused she felt. She said, "I don't like all of these tubes. I just want my mommy. I want my mommy. I want to go home." When I hear and see Spirit, it is as if I am the radio, and Spirit is the radio station. I try to dial into a strong station—and sometimes it takes a lot of adjusting to do so. But I am only the radio. If someone listens to the radio and hears beautiful music, people do not applaud the mechanical radio—they admire the musician. I am just a messenger.

I asked the group if they could identify this Spirit. Most of them shook their heads and said no. Finally, a shy Hispanic woman raised her hand and said, "I think I know this child. Her name is Marianna Martinez. She rode her pony in a parade. Something startled the pony, and she was thrown off of him. She had a terrible brain injury. She only lasted about twenty-four hours and then passed away. It was horrible. This happened twenty years ago. Her mother and I were very good friends, but we haven't been in touch for years."

What? Shy lady, you were in my group yesterday, and you did not say a word? I've been sweating buckets up here! The information was a perfect fit. My classmates felt almost as relieved as I did—then they clapped. And my migraine headache? That headache evaporated like rain in the desert, because it was not actually my headache—it was Marianna's, which she passed to me in an attempt to get my attention. She tried to tell me that she was present. She could not reach me any other way, except by showing me how horribly her head hurt after her pony threw her.

Marianna somehow found me, a complete stranger but a blinking beacon, and she made use of my gift to relay a message back to her mother. I do not know if the shy woman delivered Marianna's message; mediumship is odd enough for friends and family, let alone risking playing "telephone" with a third hand message. But I'm quite certain that, regardless, Marianna will continue to try again to reach across and comfort her mother, right up to the very day that her mother joins her across the veil. Like Katrina's mother, she was—and likely still is—on a mission. I considered this story as I finished planting the tulips, musing on mothers and daughters and grief.

My stiff joints stood me upright. It was time to clean up. The brown Georgia bats started their nocturnal sojourn and dotted the evening sky. They too seemed beautiful and miraculous. Even though I was battling cancer, and even though I still missed my own loved ones, everything felt sacred. The cold water sputtered from the garden hose and chased the dirt from my hands. I realized something both unsettling and soothing. The reality I knew was no longer the reality that I know.

Because here is the truth: love is the spiritual adhesive that permanently cements us together. When the physical body dies, it is no longer needed; it is cast aside. But our spirits prevail. And the love we exchange is the energy that connects us forever. The spectrum of love's energy, the rainbow web that connects us, appears across the veil to allow us to commune with our beloveds.

Your loved ones are around all of the time. In their experience, they haven't left, so they never want you to grieve for them. This is what motivates them to use any medium available to make contact with you—their beloved. Your loved one waits for any possible opportunity to make contact with you. Spirit wants to ease your suffering. Spirit wants to provide you with evidence-based messages to help liberate your pain. And Spirit is relentless in this attempt.

This is because Spirit knows something that most of the living do not: Spirit doesn't ever die. Our connections of love, therefore, do not sever; what severs is the mechanism that attaches us to our incarnate being. When our souls inhabit our bodies, the two are tethered together. In many ways, it's like an infant's umbilical cord ties it to the placenta—they are bound to each other, until suddenly they're not. Except in this case, it is not life that severs the cord. In this case, it is physical death.

When we die, our spiritual umbilical cord that tethered our Spirit to our physical body separates. How fascinating that physical birth and death are so similar. When we are born, the physical umbilical cord that tethered us to our mother is no longer need. Typically, when an infant's cord is cut, there is no pain. And so it is when we die. Our spiritual umbilical cord that anchored us to our body is severed—naturally. The body dies and is cast aside. Our Spirit is set free. Finally, our Spirit is untethered.

CHAPTER 8

Believe

> Life shrinks or expands in proportion to one's courage.
> —*Anaïs Nin*

Flesh curled and uncurled. Clenched and unclenched. My tongue and lips formed ugly words as I yelled, "I'm done! Do you hear me? I don't want this job anymore. I've been made fun of, disbelieved, and discredited. And now, because of you, I am publicly humiliated. I feel so betrayed. Are you guys allowed to do that? Why did I ever believe in this stuff?" Spirit was silent, so I grabbed another tissue to dry my tears.

In my final declaration, I screamed, "I quit!"

My resignation from Spirit communication started with Super Bowl Sunday of 2017. Though I've always struggled with belief, it turns out the Super Bowl was one in a series of tests that stretched my belief to its very limit. Before I tell you more, you need to know that I do not follow football. Being with family and friends and all the great food is fun—but the actual game I leave for sincere enthusiasts. I did not even know what teams were going to play until the day before the game.

That morning, my husband and I drank coffee and watched the news. As we watched the pregame hype, Spirit gave me a message, calmly stating, "The New England Patriots will win the game today; they are going to cream the Atlanta Falcons." I chuckled to myself; Spirit really emphasized the word *cream* to describe how big of a win it would be.

I had no idea why Spirit would deliver such a message to me. Not only was the message not of great spiritual importance, it was delivered to me, a non-football follower. I said to my husband, "Hey, honey, I just got a download—Spirit just told me that the Patriots are not only going to win the Super Bowl today, but they told me that they're going to 'cream' the Falcons."

I thought that telling Robin was enough, but Spirit chattered on. "You need to go public with the outcome of this game; you need to post it on Facebook. You need to post that we have told you which team will win."

What? Telepathically, I told Spirit, "No! No way! Don't ask me to put myself out there like that! I'm already under fire from nonbelievers—and now you're asking me to post a public prediction on Facebook? What if I misinterpreted you guys? I don't know enough yet; I'm still learning how to discern your messages. Besides, people take this football stuff really seriously! No. Please don't ask me to go public yet! I can't do that. I am not doing that!"

When I resist messages from Spirit, Spirit stops talking. Spirit is not punishing me. Spirit would never do that; the beings beyond the veil are merely giving me time to think about what they said. When Spirit speaks, I hear them in my head—we communicate telepathically. The voice is not male or female. The distinguishing feature of this voice is that it is infinitely kind. I am not the best student for Spirit because I challenge them. I am embarrassed to admit this, but sometimes when I talk to Spirit, I sound like an oppositional teenaged brat. With infinite patience, they continue to teach me. If the only lesson I learn is increased patience, it's fine with me; that would equate to winning the spiritual lotto.

I considered Spirit's request. Silence turned to sound. My curiosity got me. I had to ask why they wanted me to do this. Spirit responded, "Because you need to go public with the information we give to you. You must learn to trust the information that we give—regardless of how events unfold before the final outcome. You must maintain unwavering faith in us, even when skeptics or events challenge you." Spirit knew that this request was a hundred football fields past my comfort zone. Just the thought of writing a public declaration made my palms perspire.

Considering what Spirit asked of me, I weighed the probability and thought, *How bad can it be? I have a fifty-fifty chance of being correct.*

Spirit continued with instruction. "Now go do it. Post exactly what we told you earlier. Do it now, so that many people will have time to see it before the game begins."

I sat at my computer. My heart quickened as I publicly posted exactly what Spirit told me. Immediately Facebook friends and followers had opinions. Some comments utilized humor, asking how I could root for the Patriots when I lived in Atlanta. One man became furious with my prediction—not because he held any ethical issues around my psychic ability but because he was invested in his team winning! In my defense, I gently reminded people, "Hey, I'm just the messenger! I am not responsible for the content." I felt barraged by the sting of negative responses. For the first time in my life, I could not wait for the game to begin. Now my ego was invested in the outcome.

For the first time ever, I followed the game with actual interest. But to my horror, the game did not seem to go as Spirit told me it would. In fact, it was the exact opposite. The Falcons scored repeated touchdowns. My family and friends began to text and call me. Everyone had a field day mocking my prediction. One family member called and said, "Uh, are you sure Spirits *really* talk to you? Are you watching the Falcons slam the Patriots? There is no way the Patriots can win now."

How dare Spirit give me bad data and then tell me to post it! My rage ruptured. I found the remote control under some blankets and defiantly turned the TV off. This is when my verbal toxins unleashed. Patient Spirit was silent. But I wasn't. I said, "Oh, so now you won't even talk to me?"

Moments after I told Spirit that I resigned, Robin came into the room and said, "Honey, you may want to turn the game back on—the Patriots are making a comeback." *Really? What?* And history shows the outcome: the New England Patriots did make an amazing last-minute comeback, and they defeated—or, as Spirit said, *creamed*—the Atlanta Falcons. Everyone was surprised.

Spirit's game prediction was dead-on. I, on the other hand, allowed my faith to waver. I allowed other people's doubt to increase my own. When the Super Bowl game seemed to be going in the exact opposite of what Spirit told me, I stopped believing what Spirit told me. I thought that I knew better than Spirit. As I cried and cried with painful regret at my outburst, I held the proverbial olive branch. I apologized to Spirit.

Spirit spoke. "Suzanne, you needed this experience for your next level of development. We needed to show you that, regardless of how things appear, your role is to listen and believe. We have given you so many experiences now—verifiable experiences. You are ready to go forward. You are ready. We gave you this extreme example of our accuracy because as you move forward, you will need to remember this moment. Don't doubt! Regardless of how interim events unfold, and even when the outcome seems certain, do not lose your faith. Trust the information we give. Suzanne, you must believe!" Super Bowl 2017 scored a huge hallelujah in my spiritual development.

Spirit doesn't only speak to me. In fact, it uses all of my senses to initiate communication. Often, the first sign I get is color. As I've noted before, these colors trend toward a certain segment of the color wheel; vivid cobalt blues and electric purples—colors I've never seen on the physical plane and that are truly out of this world—begin to emerge and dance beneath my eyelids. When I was a teenager, I spent time in Brazil and learned some Brazilian Portuguese. I was always taken by the word *primor,* which refers to an indescribable, divine beauty; I imagine that the colors Spirit shows me could be described as such. Other times, I see eyes. I see beautiful pairs of eyes of people unknown to me. And no, it's not scary at all.

The second sign I receive is visual flashes. Spirit rapidly flashes image after image like a slide show. If I do not understand, they slow it down and repeat the same images—over and over again. It's strange, because although I may feel impatient with myself for not getting it, Spirit has never been impatient with me. Spirit lovingly repeats any information needed to help me get the correct data. These visual flashes occur in my mind, regardless of whether my eyes are open or closed.

The third sign I get is sound. I hear them. I hear Spirit talk. I usually hear a voice, often displaying a distinct accent or repeating a phrase that indicates a cultural background. Spirit wants me to correctly interpret their country of origin—not for me but for you. This is part of the evidence they provide so that you believe. As Spirit speaks, I get a strong sense that they are on my right side.

Fourth, I physically feel things. I have felt chest pain, horrible headaches, stomach upset, drug-induced highs, and even the pain and shock of a car crash. In some of my training, my teachers helped me to understand that I can put the brakes on—this particular area really required me to set and hold boundaries. Nowadays, I am always in charge of how much I allow Spirit to provide me with physical sensory data. Every once in a while, Spirit will touch me, like that first time in the bathroom when Jack tapped me on my arm. But a light touch like that to get my attention is my personal limit. Beyond physical sensation, I'm often able to have a felt sense of Spirit's unique personality. Personalities remain the same on the both sides of the veil, and somehow, I *feel* who they were when they embodied the physical.

If your loved one was funny and gregarious while alive, they are still all of those things. They show me exactly how other people felt their energy or their personalities.

And finally, Spirit sends me scents. I smell all sorts of things. I have smelled garlic, cherry pipe tobacco, and even something as earthy as horse manure! Most commonly, and I suppose in part because I am sensitive to it, Spirit sends the smell of cigarettes. When this first started happening, it was hard for me to believe it. But then it went on to happen many times.

Sometimes I connect with the loved one of someone near me, but other times, I just communicate with my Spirit guides. We all have Spirit guides, and I've been told that most of us have quite a few. Sometimes, they are only with us a short period of time—they act on sort of an as-needed basis. Other Spirit guides remain with us for our entire lives. No question is too small to ask your guides. If you want to optimize their knowledge and love for you, you have to ask. This is because Spirit guides cannot interfere with your life unless you request it.

Spirit guides are like coaches: they cannot play the game for you, but as soon as you ask for guidance, they are right there. They always have your higher good and interest at heart. Their divine contract with God is to help guide you toward your highest good. That's it. Guides hang around in Spirit form, waiting for your invitation. You can find out their names too—ask them. Whatever name pops into your head, go with it, and then ask them to give you concrete, no-way-I-could-guessed-this evidence to help you trust what you've heard.

I know this because I tried it. I wanted to know the names of my Spirit guides. I wanted to see them too. I prayed. I meditated. I asked. One morning, I went for a walk around a lake. Heavy rain fell from the sky; no humans were in sight. I silently said, "I believe that I have a guide—maybe more than one. Can you please give me a name that I can call you?"

Immediately I heard, "Esmeralda." That sounded so fantastical that I literally laughed out loud. Although I love the name Esmeralda, it is uncommon in my subculture, and I associate it with things like formality and tradition. Leave it to me to imagine something dramatic. Relentless rain pounded my face with hard, wet pellets. My pale hands turned shades of red in objection to the dropping temperature, but I barely noticed; as I pushed my feet through deep mud puddles, my mind plodded through its own dilemma.

I wanted more. I wanted to be sure that any information I got was accurate. Brazenly, I asked Esmeralda, "Can you please provide concrete confirmation that this is really your name and not my imagination?" Nothing.

The day after I asked for my guide's name, I was shopping for flowers. As I placed the bouquet in the shopping cart, my eye caught the large cursive writing. The single word written on the cellophane wrap was *Esmeralda*.

This stuff is real.

When you ask the name of your guides, they *will* give it to you. They want you to know their name because they want you to talk to them. Shortly after this event, another guide appeared in a dream. I asked him for his name, and he both provided and confirmed it, just as Esmeralda had. I now have a strong relationship with several guides.

It's easier for me to accept spiritual guidance with evidence because, like anyone, I'm the product of a culture. And my culture maintains that it's kind of odd to speak with Spirit guides, and even more odd to speak with the dead. Some may even think that it's crazy. I don't. In part, I'm able to believe because of what I've seen; it's irrefutable. Asking for more and more evidence helps build my belief, because it works every time.

In part, I'm able to believe because I work with a rock-star psychiatrist who guides me in a professional capacity. For seven years, we have worked together and treated the same patients, and if I were crazy or psychotic, he would have told me by now—or at least stopped referring patients in my direction. When I doubt myself, I seek reassurance and ask him, "Am I crazy? Do you think the cancer has gone to my brain? If I were psychotic or having hallucinations, you would tell me, right? You would protect our patients, right?" His reassuring nod and smile say everything. I feel safe knowing that my colleagues—a shrewd team of psychotherapists and this successful psychiatrist—would speak up if they could see something I couldn't. Beyond any personal or professional obligation to me, they would intervene on behalf of our patients.

In addition to professional mentorship, I have also developed relationships with people who offer me guidance on the spiritual path—spiritual teachers and mentors who have illuminated the path ahead, in addition to formal mediumship training in workshops and seminars. Each of these people helped deepen my understanding of the Spirit world. Each of them reassured me that my experiences of Spirit communications were actually nothing unusual or to be frightened about—because in many other cultures, these events are considered normal. Although each of my teachers gifted me in their unique way, their underlying message was the same: "Believe." I wanted to believe, but I also wanted confirmation.

Confirmation came. A series of synchronistic events connected me with Johnny, the Hopi medicine man who would go on to become a mentor to me—the man the great blue heron had left a feather for. He invited me to attend the annual dance of the Kachinas in his remote village. Although I didn't fully understand the spiritual meaning of this dance, I knew it was sacred for his tribe. The medicine man hinted that after the ceremony ended, he might perform a healing ritual for my tumor-filled body. I was intrigued.

I have always felt connected to Native Americans. But growing up as a pale Anglo-Saxon woman, the only exposure I had to this world was from TV and movies, and I was unsure of what was to come. I was instructed that absolutely no cameras were permitted. No cell phone photos. And I was asked to wear a simple long skirt with no bling. I thought, *No bling?* I needed to go shopping.

A local boutique offered a few possibilities. But a boutique in Atlanta is vastly different from what the tribal women who live on the reservation in Arizona would wear. That Sunday southern sun could have boiled grits on pavement. The boutique I found was scheduled to close in forty-five minutes. My fatigued, frail frame pulled open the double front doors. Just opening the heavy doors exhausted me—but they were much more than the entrance to a boutique. Those doors metaphorically opened the portal to my next Spirit contact experience.

When I entered the boutique, a waft of cigarette smoke swirled under my nostrils. I felt furious. This should be a smoke-free store. Some clerk must be on a smoke break in a back room, or maybe outside with a door propped open. I just had chemotherapy two days earlier. Many patients experience the worst side effects in the first couple of days post-chemo. Fatigue and nausea were constant companions for me. Thank goodness for anti-nausea medication. I considered how, while cancer was trying to claim my life, whoever was smoking was potentially handing theirs away. I was struck by the ironies of everyday events.

I had selected a few possible skirts when a saleswoman approached. She smelled like cigarette smoke. Immediately, I knew she was the culprit. I felt irritable that I could smell it. I thought, *People just don't get how offensive tobacco smoke smells to a nonsmoker.* In my anger, irritability, and frustration at the cigarette smell, I told myself, *If that smell makes me vomit, I'm going to spew it all over her!* What? I could not believe my ugly thoughts. How could a person who thought such thoughts call herself a medium? Why would Spirit choose to speak through me?

Before heading to the boutique that day, I had received a phone call from my friend Debbie—the one who lost her husband, Andy, in a plane crash. I initially assumed that this was why I heard *Debbie … Debbie … Debbie* in my head as the cigarette-scented saleswoman led me to the fitting room. On the way, she noticed I was short of breath, and she asked if I was okay. I apologized and told her that I was in the middle of chemotherapy. The sales woman said, "Oh! I'm so sorry. My sister just died of breast cancer." Suddenly, Spirit was standing by my right side. The time between the saleswoman telling me this and her dead sister's appearance was a splintered second. This Spirit showed me her chocolate-brown hair and brown eyes—the physical opposite of the woman standing in front of me. I asked the saleswoman if her sister had brown, short, shoulder-length hair. She said yes. I knew I was on the right energy track.

I asked if her sister had smoked. The saleswoman responded that yes, she had. I arrogantly stated, "Well, you should probably give them up too."

She looked at me, confused, and said, "But I don't smoke."

I said, "Well somebody in here smokes because I can smell it."

The saleswoman assured me that nobody had been smoking. I asked what her sister's name was, thinking that if she answered "Debbie," it would confirm Spirit was present. The woman replied, "Hannah." I was crushed. *Hannah?*

As the cigarette smell slowly dissipated, I just wanted to get out of there. None of the skirts were suitable, and the store was about to close. The saleswoman's sister was not named Debbie—rather, I was confused after the conversation with my friend Debbie. Embarrassed, I decided it was my cue to exit. I thanked the woman—and then I nearly ran for those heavy double doors.

I was fast, but Spirit was faster. Just as my hands were on the doorknobs, I heard, "Go back. Please, please, please! Go back and tell her that I am really worried about Debbie. Tell her that she needs to mend fences with her."

I telepathically asked, "What? Who is Debbie? She said that your name is Hannah? Don't make me look foolish."

Spirit pleaded, "Please go back. Try again ..."

I was so annoyed. I didn't want to go back. My battle-fatigued body felt so weary. I wanted to go home and curl up on the couch with all of my pillows and a cold ginger ale.

But I also know the pain of grief's grip. Even the strongest person can be held emotionally hostage by grief. I wanted to help. I always do. Reluctantly, I answered, "Okay, fine. But you better give me good information!"

I found the saleswoman. She was surprised that I had returned. She asked, "Oh, did you change your mind on a skirt?"

I replied, "Uh, no, not really, but I have something to ask you. I know this is going to sound really strange, but do you know a woman with a D name, like, Debbie ... she's really important to you?"

The woman's eyes widened, and she said, "Oh. My. Gosh. Yes, Debbie is my other sister!"

I said, "Well, your sister Hannah is here, and she's really worried about Debbie. I don't know why, but Hannah is quite insistent that I deliver this message. Should I keep going? Is it okay with you?"

The woman stood perfectly still and stared at me, just like the store mannequins. Then her head full of bleached blonde hair bobbed up and down in affirmation. I took a deep breath. I said, "Hannah said that you need to spend more time with Debbie. She's saying that you need to 'mend fences' and be more patient with her."

The speechless woman looked at me like I was speaking a foreign language. She slowly stated, "This is incredible. My sister Debbie was just diagnosed with breast cancer too. We all have the gene for it." She stopped and suspiciously asked, "How do you know this? It's like you know my life. That is *exactly* what Hannah would say."

The reality of my words sunk in for her as fast as pebble thrown into a pond. "She always told me I needed to have more patience with our sister Debbie. Oh my God. This is unbelievable." The saleswoman began to cry.

I continued to deliver more information. "You and your sister Debbie had a big falling out, didn't you?" In my mind's eye, I saw that Debbie had been inappropriate with the saleswoman's husband. I decided not to tell her that—after all, we were not in private, and this was a spontaneous Spirit appearance. The woman was already emotionally shaken, and I didn't want to shake her more by bringing up the tension between her husband and Debbie. I repeated, "Hannah keeps saying that you need to mend fences … you need to mend fences. Mend fences before it's too late, because you will feel terrible guilt if you don't."

I felt someone watching us. I turned around, and the other saleswoman was absently restocking shelves while she listened. I felt self-conscious. After all, this was Atlanta, and I had just delivered a message from the dead in a retail establishment. Debbie and Hannah's sister and I hugged, and I quickly darted for the doors.

A few days later, I found a simple cotton skirt in another store. I journeyed across many states to attend the Hopi ceremony. I liked Johnny the moment I met him. I hoped that the medicine man would perform a healing ritual on me, and indeed he did—though when I initially shared my Spirit contact stories, I got no more than a quiet nod. His tribe already knows these things; my experiences must have sounded quite mundane to him. After that ceremony, Johnny and I had several telephone conversations. He became a sort of mentor for me, and he did prayer work on me every day until he passed. In exchange, I sent his people love offerings.

I also sent him exotic feathers. I collect feathers as a sign from Spirit, and Johnny had an entire underground library of feathers. We connected on this level. So when I found especially beautiful feathers, I sent them to him for the feather library. We continued our interactions, based on our phone calls and the feathers. I loved him and feel forever grateful that he allowed me into his sacred sphere.

In one of these encounters, he calmly declared, "Suzanne, you must *believe!*" His words still echo in my mind. He was right—I mistrust myself all the time. I wonder what this mediumship business is, and sometimes if it's even real. The medicine man saw that, and he held me in it. He believed.

Johnny transitioned not long before this writing. When I found out, I cried. Yes, it's true—knowing all that I know, I still grieve. In my grief, I've walked miles and miles, and Johnny became a part of that journey. In the days after his passage, I begged him to send me a sign, and I specified that I'd like the sign to come in the form of a unique feather. Days passed. No special feathers appeared during my walks. Doubt arrived, and it can spread quicker than the plague. Just like it did when I thought I mistook the saleswoman's sister Hannah for my friend Debbie. I waited for my feather, and I sat with my doubt.

But then Johnny appeared in a dream to guide me. In his typical style, he said nothing. He stood in front of me with his fierce warrior stance. Our eyes met, and Johnny handed me three feathers. The medicine man, my teacher, handed me three *iridescent* feathers.

I believe.

CHAPTER 9

Signs

> Nothing in life is to be feared; it is only to be understood. Now is the time to understand more so that we may fear less.
>
> —*Marie Curie*

Once upon a time, twin sisters journeyed to the earth through their mother's withered womb. Their mother died shortly after she ushered her lovely daughters into the world. Their father raised them and bestowed benevolence in all ways. When the girls came of age, the father felt as if he had fulfilled his duty. His heart never quite mended after his wife's death. So he knocked on heaven's door, it opened, and he joined his beloved wife across the veil. The orphaned twins blossomed like lotuses from the slough. Their humble cabin, nestled sweetly in the woods, provided them with all they needed. An old crone lived down the dirt lane, and she secretly ensured the girls' safety.

The girls never learned to feel fear because all the creatures in the forest were their friends. When they entered their sixteenth year of life, an old woodcutter knocked on their cabin door. His face held deep crevices as if they had a destination. Bushy eyebrows threatened to completely mask his eyes. But behind the unruly white hairs, gentle eyes peeked with purpose. The woodcutter said he was sick and had lost his way. He petitioned the girls to provide him with food and shelter until he felt strong enough to resume his journey. The twins nodded to each other and allowed him entrance. The sisters made special soup and bread. They retrieved ale from the cold cellar that their father had brewed for special occasions. They treated the humble woodcutter as if he were a royal guest. Because of their diligent care, he returned to stable health in a fortnight.

The day arrived for the woodcutter to resume his journey. The girls walked him to a part of the forest from which he could find his way. When the sisters returned to their cabin, they found a brown burlap pouch tied with rope. An attached note read: *To fairest sisters of the land, who helped me heal with their kind hearts and tender hands. You graced me with compassion for a full fortnight. Please accept my gift of these coins-of-gold so you might purchase things that provide you with delight. ~ The Woodcutter*

The sisters untied the rope, and gold coins fell from the burlap sack. On one side of the coin was an uncomely face of the town's governor. The other side was forged with a hatchet and a serpent. Although the girls were naïve in worldly ways, they understood the gold coins could enable them to venture from the forest to purchase things of which they'd only dreamed.

The next day, the two sisters excitedly walked the long path into the village. They held hands as they walked through the open market in the village. They whispered and giggled. They purchased special herbs, and grain, and tea, and a comb, and a brush, and dainty cloth for new dresses. Word spread through the village that the beautiful twin sisters had emerged from the woods. The townspeople were quite curious how the sisters acquired the abundant gold coins held in a dilapidated burlap sack.

The corrupt governor, Mr. Evercrewel, lived in the largest stone house in the village. His likeness was featured on the front of the gold coins; on the reverse held the hatchet and the serpent—the unspoken warning to anyone who was foolish enough to cross him. His fortune was nearly gone because he had recklessly gambled it away and purchased women with special skills. The evil governor heard rumors of the twins and their new wealth. He wanted their gold. So, Governor Evercrewel lied to the townspeople. He said that a thief, who presented himself as an honest woodcutter, had recently robbed him of a large sack of gold. He bargained with a few local men who owed him money, telling them if they retrieved his gold, he would forgive their financial debt. The men journeyed into the forest to retrieve the gold. The unprepared girls were defenseless.

The outcome of the twin sisters is not specifically known because they were never seen again. When the men gave the gold to Governor Evercrewel, the evil governor told the small army of men that they had done a wicked thing by stealing from young women and ensuring their demise. Perhaps, he mused, they should be hanged. Eventually, he told them he would let them live, but he would keep the gold and, in the interest of their crimes to society as a whole, he refused to cancel their debt.

It seemed that evil had won. But then an alchemical mystery occurred. Every time Governor Evercrewel tried to spend his ill-gotten coins, they magically morphed so his image was replaced by that of one of the sisters. When he turned the coin over, he found it held the other sister's image. Folklore suggests the old crone cast a spell on those coins to ensure the corrupt governor could never use them. Indeed he couldn't, and though he continued to live a long life surrounded by riches, he was tortured by the idea of the coins that were now worthless.

Forevermore, those gold coins were called "The Blessing and The Burden." Although the burden and the blessing are opposite to each other, they reside on the same coin. Every blessing carries her counterpart: the burden. Conversely, every burden carries her counterpart: the blessing. Neither one is more important than the other. Neither one can exist on its own.

Now that I believe, I can say unequivocally that communicating with Spirit is my blessing. Receiving signs from the other side exhilarates me; it is consecrated work. I would never ask God to revoke it. It's my sacred mission here, and I finally think I've made some headway in figuring out how it works. This blessing does come with its own set of burdens, most of which arise from the reactions of others—both overt and covert. Some people don't believe me and are mistrustful of my intentions; others believe this work is evil, or "Satan in disguise," as a discouraging woman warned me at the hair salon; and still others think I'm just crazy. Although I have dealt with these burdens at different points in my psychic-mediumistic development, I know I could never return to the person I was before I knew these truths. I would not want to. My blessing continues to blossom—allowing me to pass it on and help people heal from broken hearts.

And we are all blessed—at least, all of us that can love. This is because love is the highest vibrational energy possible. Love is of God. God is love. When we feel love for another, or act with loving intention, we express divinity in motion. Love is the closest we can come to experiencing God while still in human form. This is the blessing love bestows. Death of our loved one *appears* to sever our connection. But in truth, the energy of love cannot ever be broken. In this way, love is undoubtedly a blessing.

Of course, this blessing, too, is accompanied by a burden. The burden occurs when our beloved precedes us in death—something I also happen to know a little something about, stemming from my clinical experience. Grief's gut-wrenching pain can feel like an endless nightmare from which we cannot awaken. It becomes a cruel master that has power and control over our everyday functioning. Grief psychologically incapacitates those who experience it; the weight of their emotional experience impedes logical thought processes. This is critical to repeat. *Anyone who is grieving is not fully functioning.*

Grief falls into two categories: anticipated and sudden. When grief is anticipated, such as with a long illness or old age, many grievers do some grief work before their loved one dies. And still, return to some general stability may take two to three years. On the other hand, sudden death—also known as shock loss—can take much longer, because it becomes what is clinically known as *complicated mourning.*

Two variables contribute to complicated mourning. First, if the loss was sudden. Second, if the loss was a child—even an adult child. If both of those variables occur simultaneously, expect healing time to nearly double. Four to six years seems the average amount of time it takes to regain some emotional stability. And the definition of healing is debatable. Healing does not mean never crying or feeling sad again. From a clinical perspective, healing is measured by the following factors: a) Is the griever able to resume some previous level of functioning, such as work, socially, physically? b) Is the griever crying or experiencing depressive episodes with less frequency, intensity, duration? c) If applicable, is the griever able to use alcohol or prescribed anti-anxiety medications in moderation? d) Do family and friends' feedback suggest the griever seems to have increased coping capacity with daily living? When grievers are in treatment, we regularly assess their level of functioning to see how far they've been able to come. Often, progress is so slow that even small movements toward healing bring hope.

Hope dramatically increases when we have some type of validation that our loved ones are truly around us, know what's going on in our lives, and the divine connection cannot ever be severed. As a psychic-medium, I understand that this validation can come through sacred signs. And what you may not know is that Spirit sends us signs all the time—we just can't read them if we're not paying attention. Signs from Spirit are clever, creative, and meaningful specifically for their loved one. Love is the energy that connects everything—and because of this principle, Spirit uses that energy to send signs that they are around.

Spirit often places coins, feathers, or their initial on the ground. You may also hear a special song, experience electrical disturbances, or see serial numbers. Sometimes signs come in dreams, and other times they come on literal signs on signposts. Signs can be perceived by any of the five senses. You may feel goose bumps, tingling, or a sudden cold chill; perhaps you can see Spirit, or see a flash of movement in the periphery; you may hear your name called, or smell something like tobacco or perfume. One grandmother sent me the odor of garlic as confirmation for her granddaughter! Often, these events happen when we are thinking about them—but sometimes they are surprises.

An unknown couple stood out in the garden of our historical home and read the front sign that posted providers' names and occupation. My husband and I purchased a charming c.1840 historical home to offer multi-modality healing practices and named it Serenity House Senoia. It is thought to be the first home built in the quaint town of Senoia, Georgia, where many television shows and movies have been filmed, including the current TV series *The Walking Dead*. Visitors come from all around the world to enjoy the charm of our little town and perhaps catch a glimpse of one of the actors. It feels ironic that my practice is in an area that is more associated with *The Walking Dead* than talking to the dead! If only others knew exactly how much the dead do, indeed, walk around. I was unsure as to whether the couple in the garden were *The Walking Dead* tourists, but they stayed long enough that I decided to go out and say hello.

As it turned out, they weren't. He introduced himself as a veterinarian and his wife as a forensic scientist. They said they were exploring the area to consider relocating. Senoia was at the top of their priority list with its small hometown charm. I gave them the standard tour of Serenity. They were complimentary and appeared enthusiastic. I shared my vision for the business and somehow ended up confessing that my work in implementing this vision was stymied due to my cancer treatment. The wife gasped and confided she too was in treatment for cancer. She pointed to her wig and said she hoped her hair would return. Her husband added, "Yeah, it's been one helluva a year."

His wife responded, "It really has been hard! My poor husband has been dealing with all of my appointments and treatments and being sick—"

The husband interjected to add, "And my brother died recently too."

As soon as the man shared his brother's death, the brother appeared on my right side. He started with the typical telepathic communication and showed me pictures in my mind. Spirit telepathically said, "It was sudden, so sudden …"

I looked at the husband and said, "It was not a long illness, was it? He passed suddenly, but it wasn't a car accident …" The husband sadly shook his head as Spirit showed me a gun. It turned out this man had struggled with addiction his whole life and eventually shot himself.

Spirit continued to show me things, including the final moments of his life. I saw a dark-haired charismatic man with a big smile. The ladies wanted to be around him, and the men wanted to emulate him. His energy was big in life and just as big in death.

When our physical body dies, or crosses over, or transitions, it no longer means our personality is gone too. If someone was shy or outrageously gregarious when they were in their physical body, they carry those traits with them. No two spirits have ever felt alike. When they show up in Spirit, their personality clearly comes through. This Spirit showed me that he "danced with death" through high-risk behaviors his entire physical life. Although he had been a spiritual seeker and asked existential questions, he battled with addiction and destructive behaviors. He showed me how he twirled the cylinder on a revolver. Some chambers were loaded with bullets, others were empty. While he was under the influence, he played Russian roulette. As I watched him spinning the cylinder, I felt the familiar lightheadedness or high feeling—a clear indicator that he had been using substances.

The final time he pulled the trigger, a bullet was in the chamber. He died instantly. It was not an intentional suicide but almost more like a dare with God. He was shocked when his physical body immediately died. He showed me how he stood above his body and tried to figure out how he could get back in. But it was too late. His physical body was dead.

Spirit wanted his brother to know that he was terribly sorry. But that wasn't the most important thing to him. He had a daughter. This child was not his biological child, but he helped raise her. He adored her. He wanted his brother to check in on her—and tell her that while he did not have consistent contact prior to his death, she held his heart and was his greatest joy. He added, "She gave me the opportunity to experience being a father, and I loved it. I love her. I'm so sorry …" He felt terrible that his actions would negatively impact her life and bring her intense emotional pain.

As I delivered this information, the couple sitting in front of me confirmed every detail—yet I could still feel their skepticism. I asked the husband what he would accept as a sign that his brother was really there. He responded, "If I saw a yellow ten-speed bike in the next month, I would accept that as a sign; I would believe." He told me how he had borrowed his brother's yellow bike as a child, and I could see that the image was powerful to him. We said our goodbyes, and I walked them back through the garden and to the street.

Then the wife pointed and said, "Oh my God! There it is! That's your sign!" We looked. There was a sign, canary yellow, with a ten-speed bike on it.

The husband began to laugh and cry. He said, "Ha! My brother is still joking around! It's so funny that he actually gave me a sign in a sign!"

And I thought to myself, *This is how a skeptic begins to believe.*

Manipulating electrical appliances is another common way for Spirit to let you know that they are present. Joanne sat on the couch and cried over the recent sudden death of her husband, who she noted had been quite handy with electrical things. I checked the atomic digital wall clock to see how much time we had left for our session. Suddenly, that clock went berserk! The numbers cycled so fast they were no longer legible. Round and round numbers ran. The clock was not low on batteries. It hangs above the door where it's not easily reached, so it's highly unlikely anyone had tampered with it. We both stared at the clock spinning time. I wondered what to do; I was at work, and I never cross my psychic-mediumistic work with my role as a psychotherapist. But I quickly realized that Joanne knew exactly what was going on. She grabbed an empty chair, climbed on top, and recorded a video on her cell phone. She said, "That is my husband! He's doing that! I can't wait to show our kids this video!" That event occurred several years ago. The same ordinary clock still hangs above my office door. It has not done anything like that since.

In other cases, lights will blink, or a lightbulb will burst. Appliances will spontaneously turn on like a radio, TV, fan, lamp, or a computer. I spoke with a woman named Angela who had recently lost her beloved. One day when her grief was fresh, she got into her car and began to cry. When she turned her car on, a rather outdated song—one that had been sentimental to them both—played on the radio. Although she wanted to believe, she doubted and tested him. She said out loud, "Well, if you're really here, then make that song play again!" The song ended. She changed the station, and the same song started over again.

Our loved ones want to send us signs in any way possible, and as we begin to open the veil, these signs provide proof for the truths that are difficult for us to understand: namely, that there is no such thing as death. Spirit uses whatever resources are available to do this. Once we learn to read these signs, Spirit starts sending us messages in a different way. Learning to hear those messages takes training, but it's well worth it.

Because once we really learn to hear messages from the spirits of the dead, from animals and fetuses and everything else connected to the rainbow web, we can start to hear messages from an even greater source; we can receive direct guidance from beyond.

I first started receiving this direct guidance one early morning on the anniversary of 9/11. I decided to get my morning walk in before my husband and son awakened. As usual, I walked around the nearby golf course and onto an excavation site where the red clay had been dug to create a new reservoir for our growing community. The golfers had not teed up for the first hole, nor had anyone arrived at the construction site. I felt fortunate that nobody else was around. I love being outside, surrounded by nature, and I felt like I was in a private playground. We had not had rain in weeks. The clay appeared dry and hardened and solid, except for a few dips that held an inch or two of water. I walked toward a flock of geese with a bag of stale bread in my hand.

I hopped and jumped around the mud puddles, trying not to get my new shoes dirty. The day held so much promise. The sun worked his magic and shone bright, and the wind held her tongue and blew just enough breeze to make humans comfortable. I marveled in the splendor of life. I hopped to the next spot. The geese looked over at me and understood I was coming.

I stepped onto another patch of earth. The top layer was hard and cracked open from the hot sun. It reminded me of chicken pot pie, with the cracked top crust. I started to sink a little—and when I tried to get the sinking foot free, it would not release. I jiggled it several times, but it just sank further. I had to bring my other foot next to the sinking foot to maintain my balance. In seconds,

I sank from the tops of my athletic shoes to my ankles. *You should be glad that nobody is around to see you … you look ridiculous,* said my inner skeptic-bitch. I looked around. Not a soul in sight. I was grateful to be unseen. I tried to extract my feet from the mud. Instead of setting myself free, I sank more! *How foolish of me to not have carried my phone,* I thought initially. Later, as I sank, I realized I would not have had time to dial a number anyway.

Cold, gritty mud clung to me and dragged me further down some bottomless hole. *This is crazy! Where's the bottom? How could this be so deep? We haven't had rain in weeks.* The earth had appeared solid. *Panic. I can't feel the bottom.* I could not find anything solid below to push against for leverage. *Is this quicksand? We don't have quicksand in Georgia, right? Why did you have to go out this early, when nobody is around? So silly, Suzanne …* Now the mud monster claimed my calves. It was thick like cold mucus. My skin itched, but I had no time to think about itchiness. I could still swivel my hips, so I turned my head in all directions. Even if I screamed, nobody would hear me. I did not see a single solitary soul. I had taken early-morning walks in the area for years, and I knew that there was typically a course keeper tending the greens before the course opened. Where was he now? Instead of feeling embarrassed, now I felt desperate. In an effort to boost my internal morale, I reminded myself that I am former military. *I am strong! I got this. I can extricate myself—just try harder—maybe just move one leg at a time.*

Sink. Cold. Wet. Sand.

The geese stared at me. I still held the half loaf of stale bread in my right hand. My inner skeptic-bitch sarcastically stated, *Oh, good little soldier, you, still holding their bread … maybe you'll get an award …* Further and further and further I sank. Colder and colder, the mud threatened to consume the whole of me. Suction now. My shoes were being sucked off of my feet! Every time I tried to lift my foot, I felt suction pulling at me. Maybe if my shoes came off, I could be more mobile, and I could get out. But I could not get my legs to meet. I could not work a shoe off. I could not help the earth suck my shoes from my feet. I was now up to my thighs. I began to wonder when they'd find my body. *What an embarrassing way to die, Suzanne,* cackled my inner skeptic-bitch. Horrified, I considered that they may not find it until after they filled the lake. *What an asinine way to go out.* The earth was very cold, and my legs quickly lost feeling and sensation.

Just as the mud reached the bottom curve of my butt, a voice I did not know spoke telepathically: "Stop struggling. Stop moving. Distribute your weight, Suzanne! Bend over at your waist. Spread out your arms in front of you. Reach across the top. Distribute your weight. Stop moving. Be still. Do it now!" This voice was much kinder than my inner skeptic-bitch and nearly as convincing.

Terrified, I placed my arms up and out and stretched them as far as I could across the soil in front of me. Everything was still. Miraculously, I stopped sinking! *You're not out yet,* inner skeptic-bitch taunted.

But the unknown, new voice clearly said, "Slowly, Suzanne, move very, very slowly and continue to reach out in front of you. As you distribute your weight, you will be able to slowly wiggle one leg at a time to break the suction. Slowly." My entire chest was flat across the soil. I kept my arms stretched out in front of me and floated on the cold, wet mud; there was nothing solid within reach. As I continued to listen to the kinder voice, I stopped fighting the suction beneath me. Instead of resisting, I allowed. Then very slowly, gently, I wiggled one leg and the other, centimeters at a time.

I felt a release. I was determined now to set myself free. As I pulled my freezing legs from the earth, I reverted to my military training and elbow-crawled all of the way to the land's edge. My body trembled and shook. I looked like a walking mud puddle— but I was alive.

This was one of those trust-us-now-or-die moments. We all have the ability to receive spiritual guidance from the other side. Part of our lesson here on earth is to learn to trust that guidance, and that starts with believing it's real. It also requires us to believe that the voices we hear truly want the best for us. *Your Spirit guides never, ever give bad advice or suggest harm to yourself or anyone else.* Spirit guides always—always and in all ways—speak from pure love to help us in our time of need. Developing a relationship with them requires being open to the many signs they send. Once you've managed to do that sufficiently, you can enter into direct conversation with not only the dead but a type of Spirit greater than that. This is the true blessing that comes with mediumship.

Many people who don't experience mediumship themselves can still benefit from understanding it, because it will be there to comfort them in their time of need—they need only believe. Experiencing love of another is a sacred blessing. It's truly a divine experience. But losing our loved one to physical death is a burden so big it crushes the strongest of hearts. That's the burden that comes with death. Here, mediumship offers us the opportunity to alleviate that burden, if we can only believe what seems unbelievable: that *they are not really dead.* Because we don't die. We are spiritual beings experiencing human form. And when we consciously accept mediumship as a real phenomenon, then we exercise that blessing in its fullest form; between life and death, we form a bridge.

In my case, I'm a bridge in more ways than one. My knowledge bridges an understanding of grief and psychosis and an understanding of mediumship. At the same time, my body stands squarely on the bridge between life and death; though I'm alive, death is always at my side. My body endures repeated painful procedures to treat metastatic cancer, and that pain nudges me to be ever mindful of time—the time I have and the time I don't. It's a visceral reminder that my own untethering between the physical and spiritual creeps closer.

My cousin once said to me, "Suzanne, the little bird of death rests on your shoulder." And while a little bird is a feather-light creature, the proximity of death feels like an albatross around my neck. My own painstaking experiences of shock loss broke me wide open. That break nearly killed me. Then came cancer, which is trying to kill me still. But now I truly know that death is an event that takes place in the body, not the Spirit. Spirit cannot die. Grief creates relentless yearning and unfulfilled aching to be reunited, but this pain is unnecessary. Because our loved ones who have transitioned are just a breath away. It's so beautifully simple.

Love is the spiritual plasma that forever binds us. This spiritual plasma is so much stronger than any physical tether. Though my fierce will fights to remain in my physical body, living with dozens of cancerous tumors is like having a terrorist living in your house: the situation is dangerously unpredictable.

This collection of Spirit contact stories reflects my journey, which forced me to plough through proverbial tsunamis and floods and one-way roads. I marched through inhospitable terrain—and I cursed every step. I crawled on my hands and knees toward any possible safe place. But crawl I did—with jagged fingernails and bloody elbows and torn knees. I crawled. I crawled toward survival and growth. Although I did not know it then, I now know that I needed to survive *precisely because* I had to share these true events with you. I had to tell you that I have seen spirits, just like your own loved ones. I have seen hundreds of spirits who departed their physical body and exist now as pure Spirit. These beautiful spirits have a message for you:

They are not dead.

Four years have passed since I experienced my first contact with Spirit. I continue to live on the edge of life and death. I have written and rewritten these final pages, working and reworking them to bring this book to you. I did this because my own words didn't speak to me—so how could they speak to you? Now I know why. Because the thing that was supposed to happen hadn't happened yet. My own story. My own story line was still unfolding.

As I sit at my computer, it's mid-January 2018. I'm still in my nightgown. I look outside at the leafless trees that appear dead. My eyes are red and puffy again; because of previous cancer treatment, the tissue around the eye is extremely sensitive and flares easily. A recent kidney infection healed. That feels better. But my back is a problem.

My back is up against the wall—I'm out of options. I hate being a woman without options. The hourglass that measures time drains right in front of my eyes. Some things you just don't get to turn over and begin again. Like this hourglass. So it is with a spinal tumor.

My back hurt. For several months, my back felt like a horse kicked me right in my spine. I thought it was a pulled muscle. But the pain. God the pain. At times, I ended up in a fetal position sobbing. No physical position or heat or cold or over-the-counter medications completely stopped the excruciating pain. Now I know why. My spine is broken.

Eight months ago, while writing this book, I completed radiation to the cancerous tumor inside of the T-7 vertebrae. The radiation made that bone brittle. The tumor, it appears, did not die—it just grew bigger. That tumor is pushing through the broken bone. Both the tumor and broken bone are impinging on my spinal cord. The relentless pain is a constant reminder to get this story told. Surgery is scheduled in a few weeks. The reason for the delay is that my white blood cell count is "in the tank," as the nurse noted. A low white blood cell count means the body does not have many good soldiers left to fight off any bad guys or infections. This is important because this surgeon's plan is to secure my entire spine. It involves being in the OR for nine hours—and trying to scrape the spinal tumor from the broken spine without compromising my spinal cord.

So, this book may be published posthumously. I don't know. But what Spirit has shown me is that it doesn't matter—because only love is real.

My own journey has taken me through the emotional, fecal-filled trenches of sudden death, or shock loss, and rounds of cancer. The universe, in her infinite wisdom, wastes nothing. Everything gets recycled—not just physical, tangible things but our experiences too. It's the great circle of life. So, my previous traumas and upcoming surgery are my greatest teachers. These teachers pulled back the invisible veil so that I could see Spirit. My seeing Spirit is my spiritual gift for the collective.

I say it's for the collective because I still don't see my loved ones on the other side—I see yours. Because of this, what I know is *we do not die*.

I sit on the precipice of life and death. Dwindling options force me to focus on what is real. What is real is Spirit. Death is an illusion. And your loved ones in Spirit work very hard to communicate messages as evidence of their continued existence. These messages are the spiritual gift that rightfully belongs to you. Accept the gift.

Six months before I was diagnosed with terminal cancer, I started to see dead people, or Spirit—because all of the world conspired to convert me, an average housewife and mother, to a psychic-medium. This story is for you.

APPENDIX
Common Questions about Spirit Contact

The appendix addresses the skepticism and natural curiosity that many people have about mediumship. Designed as an easy reference guide, readers can flip to this appendix to address their concern or satisfy their curiosity.

Is there a difference between a medium and a psychic?

Yes. Everyone has psychic ability to a certain degree. A medium has the ability to mediate between the world of the living and Spirit. Every medium is psychic, but not every psychic is a medium.

My loved one was killed in a horrible accident. Did they suffer?

No. We are never meant to suffer. Though some of us die with physical pain, death itself brings only relief from that pain. We stand outside of our bodies and may watch the final moments of our "death," but we are surrounded by heavenly beings and other family members or important people who have already transitioned. They lovingly stand with us in a difficult death, such as accident or murder. We do not suffer.

How do our loved ones find us?

Everything is energy. Love is the energy that binds us like heavenly duct tape! When my dead brother appeared to our mother in a dream, he took her over to the window and showed her a magnificent spectrum of light. He said, "You see that, Mom? That's how I find you. That spectrum of light is the energy of love between us."

Do all Christians, Jews, Muslims, Hindu, and other faiths go to the same place after death?

Yes! We all go home to the same place: we return home to God. It doesn't matter what faith we were while here—or even if someone was an atheist. (And boy, are atheists ever surprised!) This is not my opinion but my experience through spirits from every religion, faith, and belief system.

Is it important to pray?

Yes! Our prayers are always heard. I understand prayer can change the outcome of events. Although I do not understand why some prayers appear to be answered while others appear to not be answered.

What advice would you have for those of us who would like to be in direct communication with our spirit guides?

Pray, meditate, ask. Our guides wait for our invitation to connect and guide and help. Begin by asking for a name you should call them. Then listen to what names pop into your mind and ask for confirmation. Spirit guides cannot interfere with our life— we do have free will. But as soon as we ask them, help comes immediately.

Do you feel people are given a gift of insight, or is this something that can be fostered and found in each of us? As in, if we practiced and opened ourselves, could there be more of us able to hear from the spirit world?

I agree with many other well-known mediums who have said that the best mediums are born with the gift, and it appears to run in families. That said, we can all open up to spirit guidance through meditation and prayer.

I'm grieving over my loved one's death. How do I correctly communicate to them?

Start talking! The great news is that there isn't any secret code or language to communicate with your loved one. They know every time you say their name, write them a letter, or talk out loud.

Does everyone that passes away have a spirit that can be contacted?

Everyone has a spirit and every life form. We can invite or ask a loved one to come to us through a sign, appearance, or a dream. Sometimes they are not immediately (after they transition) available, for reasons I'm not completely clear about. However, when they can, they will make every attempt to make their presence known to you.

Do spirits have a life span?

Yes. Spirits have a life span: infinity. We are pure divine energy, and therefore, spirits are forever.

Do you believe our loved ones that passed contact us by showing up in other living things?

Yes! Spirit will ask other life forms, birds, and butterflies to help them get a message to you. Can you imagine the honor it is for the animals to give such a gift? They too are doing God's work.

How are our spirit guides determined? Are they loved ones from past lives or just a spirit who might be up for the challenge?

As far as I know, our guides are typically loved ones we've known before, and as part of their spiritual development, they agree to become like a coach on the other side. It's my understanding that they can't ever interfere with our life unsolicited, but as soon as we ask, they joyfully assist. I often see grandparents who tell me they are the spirit guide for the person in front of me.

Once you have seen and communicated with someone's loved one, do you see them every time you see that person?

No. I do not see most people's loved ones every time I see them. However, for some people, their loved ones show up repeatedly! I'm unsure why. But it feels as if that spirit's energy is more forceful or a big personality—or they really want to get a message across to their loved one.

If I have a dream in which my departed loved one appeared, is it just a dream or something more?

It depends. Sometimes we dream of our loved ones and it's a dream—but in general, dreams are one of the most common methods through which your loved one can communicate! One way to help you discern is ask yourself, *how real did it feel?* When Spirit appears in a dream, it's palpable. Their visit is typically very brief with a message of love, but you awaken from it with a gut knowing, as if you really did just see your loved one in the flesh.

If I would like a psychic reading, how do I find a good medium that I can trust?

Word of mouth seems to be the best way. You can Google well-known evidential mediums. Remember that a valid psychic/medium would *never* provide harmful information, call for violence or retaliation, or recommend anything that would go against God.

I always get nervous when I think about going to a psychic/medium. I worry that they are fake and will tell me what they think I want to hear. I hate being such a skeptic. Any words of advice?

Hang on to your skepticism and your critical discernment. Many fakes exist. This line of work invites charlatans who will gladly take your money and tell you what they think you want to hear. There are also many well-meaning people who have some gifts but are not able to provide solid evidence. After all, even authentic psychics/mediums are at different developmental levels. Some are truly gifted and have received training, while others have just one or the other. Always trust your own intuition first!

Do spirits say the same thing?

Oftentimes, Spirit will want to tell me details of their life or death, or pass on a message about their loved one's life that they could not deliver when they were alive. As you've read in this book, Spirit reveals their personality in a myriad of ways. But overall, there is really only one message: love. Only love is real, and love provides the map that leads Spirit back to the ones we've left behind. If we miss them, we need only love them, and they will appear. Truly, it's universal.

"Can we communicate with our deceased loved ones? This has been one of humankind's most enduring questions. *Spirit Untethered* brings a new and exciting perspective to this ancient question. Suzanne Grace Maiden is extraordinary. While battling a life-threatening malignancy, she courageously shares important new evidence that we don't really die. Suzanne presents her many experiences of encountering the deceased with messages for their loved ones. With each turn of the page, you will find a treasure trove of insights and inspiration. This outstanding book is expertly written, remarkably easy to read, and enthusiastically recommended."

—Jeffrey Long, MD, author of the New York Times best-selling Evidence of the Afterlife: The Science of Near-Death Experiences

"*Spirit Untethered* explores a tender journey as a psychotherapist diagnosed with terminal cancer which ultimately opened her spiritual eyes. It provides hard-hitting evidence that we never die and our loved ones always reach back to comfort us. A must-read."

—Mark Anthony the Psychic Lawyer®, and author of Evidence of Eternity

"Get ready to laugh, cry, and be thoroughly entertained by this spiritual page-turner. Not only does Suzanne Maiden tell captivating stories of her dance with cancer and the sudden gift for mediumship that accompanied her illness but she lands the reader squarely on the doorstep of deep truth—what connects us all in life and beyond is the web of love. And whether a soul is tethered to a body or taking flight, she gently reminds us, even as she faces her own mortality, that only love is real. An outstanding book destined to inspire, comfort, and awaken us all to what really matters."

—Lori Lothian, creator of The Awakened Dreamer blog

"As is true for me, anyone who knows Suzanne Maiden has already experienced *her* untethered spirit in the most authentic and transparent way. She exudes love, grace, and gratitude in every aspect of her life, and if possible, even more so since living with her cancer diagnosis and the unique challenges she has encountered as a result. Her book, *Spirit Untethered*, is born of her journey inward and her passionate desire to share those transformative experiences with the reader. She reveals her connection with the spirit world in a uniquely honest and courageous unfolding of occurrences that leaves you searching your own soul for connection with your loved ones past and present. Knowing Suzanne has changed my life, and her book: the way I embrace it."

—*Mary Ann Navarre, MA, licensed professional counselor*

"What a perfect title *Spirit Untethered* is for Suzanne Maiden's book. I would not wish on anyone the pain and agony of the many surgeries she's had in dealing with metastatic cancer. At the same time, this ordeal has been a kind of gift, not only to her but to us, her readers. The challenges of coping with cancer have propelled her into the non-ordinary realm of communication with the spirit world and the palpable certainty of the supremacy of love. Her book is filled with inspiring stories of mediumistic incidents that challenge us to expand our awareness to trust that death is not the end."

—*David Van Nuys, PhD, emeritus professor of psychology, creator/host of "The Shrink Rap Radio" podcast*

"I have had the honor of knowing Suzanne for the last couple of years, though it feels like a lifetime of sisterhood. She is simply amazing in her ability to share her gifts of Spirit clearly, beautifully, and, most importantly, with an open heart. One of my favorite stories is a sharing that took place with my husband.

She connected with his younger brother who had recently passed. The evidence and healing that were shared in that message was truly touching and brought peace to my husband's grieving heart. I love her!"

—Cathy Sackett, *intuitive counselor, psychic, and medium*

"I have had the privilege of bearing witness to Suzanne's deep, intense and authentic journey of transformation that has opened her inner eyes, ears, and heart to the living presence of the other world and its spirit inhabitants. Facing the grimmest diagnosis that has pushed her beyond the threshold of the personal life, she has been opened to the message of enduring love that steadily comes through, unbidden, to give life meaning, hope, integrity, and a great continuity and relatedness with all things."

—Barry S. Williams, M. Div., PsyD,
Diplomate Jungian analyst, mara'akame

"It is no surprise that Suzanne can communicate with the deceased. She is a bright light, a vivacious cosmic energy and a fearless spirit. I have known Suzanne for well over a decade and have always respected her impeccable resolve to live life fully, joyfully and in passionate service to others. Now as she journeys with life threatening cancer, the portal to the world of spirit is open. Untethered Spirit is a gem of a book, a joy to read, with an essential message that when we die, our loving doesn't die, and that loving has a clear and sassy voice through the veil of life and death."

—Jenny Suzumoto, *MA Spiritual Director*

"It was during dinner at Thai Spice in Peachtree City, Georgia, that Suzanne asked me a question. Over spicy curries and Pad

Thai with our spouses, Suzanne leaned in and asked permission to share with me messages from my brother. Brett had passed away in April at the age of forty-six, and I had been dealing with his passing. Brett had cerebral palsy, unable to speak and confined to a wheelchair. I took care of him growing up, feeding, bathing, and clothing him. He wasn't supposed to live past his teens, yet he outlived our parents. It was during this dinner that Suzanne, who didn't know anything about my family, proceeded to give me messages from Brett. Messages that meant so much, perfect timing to my mourning. I hadn't shared his passing, yet Suzanne described in jaw-dropping detail particulars that stunned me. Perfect messages at the most needed time. Her care in wording, her delivery was nothing short of love … from the other side."

—*Jerry C., retired police investigator*

"I have personally witnessed Suzanne's spontaneous readings on several occasions. At each reading, she revealed personal details about the person for whom she had no prior knowledge. It is amazing to watch her in action. She is the real deal!"

—*Liz Western, teacher*

"Upon hearing this podcast, I was quite moved by Suzanne's interview with Dr. Dave. Despite my atheistic leanings, I felt a sense of curiosity and openness to her sense of connectedness to the divine.

My significant other was killed in a bicycle accident about a month ago, and this loss has spurred in me a wish for a connection with the afterlife in ways I never before experienced.

As a result of hearing this interview, I contacted Suzanne and arranged for a reading. She was lovely—down to earth, very present, very realistic in many ways, and yet offered up information that was both accurate and insightful about my partner and our connection. I found this immensely helpful during this difficult time of grief, and although I still feel that the mystery of the afterlife is something we can't fully embrace or understand in this life as we know it, it was wonderful to hear Suzanne's sensitive comments and feelings of connectedness. I appreciated what she shared with me very much.

I would recommend her highly—and I imagine she is also a very good psychotherapist, given her compassionate and insightful nature."

—Selena Mitchell, small business owner

"This message is for any doubters who think you may be a fake and just make up these stories for personal gratification. I consider myself a realist. I have never believed in spirits or the ability of one to foresee future events. I have known you and your family for the past twelve years or so. I have heard you tell these stories before, but until recently, they were just stories. You, Suzanne, are the real deal. There is no doubt in my mind that you have the ability to see spirits and have a knack of foreseeing future events. You are an amazing, beautiful, loving, giving, caring person, and I am honored to know you. I sincerely hope with all my heart that anyone who has any doubt of your abilities knows that you are truly the real deal!"

—Sherry Duckett, medical assistant

CPSIA information can be obtained
at www.ICGtesting.com
Printed in the USA
LVHW021046291218
602142LV00001B/160/P